GRAMMAR IN PRACTICE

Usage

Lesli J. Favor, Ph.D.

AMSCO SCHOOL PUBLICATIONS, INC.
315 HUDSON STREET, NEW YORK, N.Y. 10013

Cover Design: Meghan J. Shupe
Cover Art: picturequest.com/Brand X Pictures
Text Design: Nesbitt Graphics, Inc.
Compositor: Nesbitt Graphics, Inc.

When ordering this book, please specify: *either* **R 018 W** *or*
GRAMMAR IN PRACTICE: USAGE

Please visit our Web site at: ***www.amscopub.com***

ISBN 978-1-56765-134-8
NYC Item 56765-134-7

PRINTED IN THE UNITED STATES OF AMERICA

6 7 8 9 10   10 09

About the Author

Lesli J. Favor loves grammar! She began her career in education as a writing tutor at the University of Texas at Arlington. After earning her BA in English there, she earned her MA and Ph.D. at the University of North Texas. While there, she taught courses in composition and literature. Afterward, she was assistant professor of English at Sul Ross State University-Rio Grande College. Now, as an educational writer, she is the author of fourteen books for young adult readers and students. She lives in the Seattle area with her husband, two dogs, and a horse.

Consultants

Nancy Mae Antrim is an assistant professor of English and Linguistics at Sul State University. Her Ph.D. is in linguistics from the University of Southern California. Prior to completing her doctorate, she taught ESL at Riverside High School in El Paso, Texas. Currently her teaching and research interests involve language teaching and methodology and second language acquisition. She has presented her research at numerous national and international conferences.

Gary Pankiewicz has been teaching high school English for ten years at Hasbrouck Heights High School in Bergen County, New Jersey. He received his BA and MA (with a concentration in Composition Studies) from Montclair State University.

for Kathryn Rogers,
grammar goddess

Contents

Introduction: How to Use This Book—and Why   vii

PART 1   REFRESH YOUR MEMORY _____ 1

Lesson 1   The Eight Parts of Speech   2

Lesson 2   Review of the Eight Parts of Speech   12

Real-World Applications: Parts of Speech   16

Test Practice: Parts of Speech   18

PART 2   USING GRAMMAR AND THE MECHANICS OF WRITING _____ 21

Lesson 3   Using Verbs   22
Using the Correct Tense   22
Principal Parts of Verbs   26
Agreement of Subject and Verb   30
Five Troublesome Verb Pairs   34

Lesson 4   Using Nouns   39
Concrete Nouns and Abstract Nouns   39
Collective Nouns   40
Count and Noncount Nouns   42

Lesson 5   Using Modifiers   46
Articles, Demonstratives, and Quantifiers   47
Degrees of Comparison   49
Adjectives and Adverbs Confused   54
Double Negatives   56
Other Problems   57

Lesson 6   Using Pronouns   59
Personal Pronouns   59
Agreement of Pronoun and Antecedent   62
Intensive and Reflexive Pronouns   63
Indefinite Pronouns   65

Lesson 7   Review of Using Verbs, Nouns, Modifiers, and Pronouns   70

Real-World Applications: Using Grammar   75

Lesson 8   Using Punctuation   77

Lesson 9   Using Capitalization   84

Lesson 10   Using Spelling   90
    Frequently Misspelled Words 95
    Words Often Confused 97
    Abbreviations and Numbers 99

Lesson 11   Review of Using Grammar and Mechanics   100

Real-World Applications: Using Grammar and Mechanics   105

Test Practice: Using Grammar and Mechanics   107

PART 3   PHRASES AND CLAUSES _____ 111

Lesson 12   The Prepositional Phrase   112
    Adjective Phrases 113
    Adverb Phrases 115

Lesson 13   The Verbal Phrase   122
    Gerund Phrases 123
    Participial Phrases 125
    Infinitive Phrases 128

Lesson 14   Main and Subordinate Clauses   132
    The Main Clause 133
    The Subordinate Clause 134
    Uses of Subordinate Clauses 137

Lesson 15   Using Phrases and Clauses as Modifiers   144
    Misplaced Modifiers 145
    Dangling Modifiers 148

Lesson 16   Review of Phrases and Clauses   153

Real-World Applications: Phrases and Clauses   161

Test Practice: Phrases and Clauses   163

PART 4   THE FOUR SENTENCE TYPES _____ 167

Lesson 17   The Simple Sentence   168

Lesson 18   The Compound Sentence   171

Lesson 19   The Complex Sentence   175

Lesson 20   The Compound-Complex Sentence   179

Lesson 21   Review of Sentence Types   184

Real-World Applications: Sentences Types   189

Test Practice: Sentence Types   191

Test Practice: Grammar, Mechanics, Phrases,
                   Clauses, and Sentences   194

Glossary   *198*
Index   *201*

INTRODUCTION
How to Use This Book
—and Why

A thorough understanding of grammar and the mechanics of writing is one of the pillars of a solid education. It prepares you for success in college, careers, and daily life. For this reason, now more than ever, students are being asked to demonstrate proficiency in grammar, usage, and composition. State tests, the SAT, and the ACT will measure your ability to recognize and correct errors in grammar and mechanics. These tests as well as your classroom assignments require that you write clear, correct sentences and paragraphs, both in isolation and in essay format.

This is the second in a series of books that offer instruction, review, and practice in the basics of grammar, mechanics, and composition. The concepts build on one another, from the parts of speech through paragraph composition, so that by the end of the series, you will have the tools necessary to assemble polished compositions. The first book, *Grammar in Practice: A Foundation,* covered the parts of speech, grammar rules, punctuation, capitalization, and spelling. This book offers expanded instruction on grammar, common usage errors, and using different kinds of sentences. The next book, *Grammar in Practice: Sentences and Paragraphs,* will show you how to pull together your grammar and usage skills to write strong, engaging sentences and paragraphs.

Here in *Grammar in Practice: Usage* you will find a variety of lessons, features, and activities:

- **Instructional sections:** Short, easy to read sections introduce and explain key concepts, complete with definitions, explanations, and examples. Your teacher may skip sections you already know well and return for review to sections that were especially helpful or important.

- **Activities:** Many brief workbook-style exercises let you practice applying lesson concepts. Some are literature-based exercises that require critical analysis of specific points of grammar, mechanics, or style in an excerpt.

- **Composition Hints:** These features offer tips and techniques for applying rules and for developing your personal style in writing.

- **ESL Focus:** These features explain points of grammar and usage that can be particularly challenging to non-native English speakers.

- **Writing Applications:** To help you integrate the grammar and usage concepts you learn, you'll often be asked to write and revise sentences and paragraphs, occasionally working with a classmate.

- **Games and Puzzles:** Throughout the book you will find visual puzzles and word games that will reinforce what you're learning. They offer a fun yet challenging way to approach grammar and usage. Depending on the puzzle, your teacher may have you work in pairs or may provide hints or word lists derived from the teacher's manual.

- **Real-World Applications:** These assignments at the end of each lesson group let you explore how people use grammar, mechanics, and sentences in the real world, outside classroom walls. With them, you'll have the opportunity to showcase your strengths while incorporating your individual style and creativity. Many of them feature technology applications.

- **Test Practice:** Each lesson group concludes with a practice test covering only the material in those lessons. Additionally, the book concludes with a comprehensive test covering major concepts in the book. Most tests are multiple choice and are modeled after state-proficiency and standardized tests you will take in order to graduate or apply to colleges.

With so much variety, this book is an invaluable tool. Your teacher can pick and choose lessons, work through from beginning to end, or have you use the book as a homework resource. However you and your teacher decide to use it, you'll learn how to craft stronger sentences that are free of grammar errors. Use the entire series and you will be able to write interesting and effective compositions with confidence and flair.

Lesli J. Favor, Ph.D.
Author

Auditi Chakravarty
Editor

Parts of Speech: Refresh Your Memory

As you know, a word may play one of eight parts in a sentence.

1. noun
2. pronoun
3. verb
4. adjective

5. adverb
6. preposition
7. conjunction
8. interjection

 These eight parts are known as the *parts of speech.*

We use the eight parts of speech to build sentences that are grammatically correct. In this book, the first two lessons help you review the eight parts of speech and their uses in sentences. Then, in lessons to follow, you will find detailed guidelines for using the parts of speech and troubleshooting grammatical errors in sentences.

The Eight Parts of Speech

All sentences are built using a combination of the eight parts of speech.

The Eight Parts of Speech

PART OF SPEECH	WHAT IT DOES	EXAMPLE
noun	It names a person, place, thing, animal, or idea. *Proper nouns* name particular persons, places, etc., and are capitalized.	writer, family, story, salesperson, amazement, self-control Gregor Samsa, Europe
pronoun	It takes the place of a noun. An *antecedent* is the noun that a pronoun stands for.	he, she, it, I, mine, everyone *Gregor* dislikes *his* job.
verb	It expresses action (action verb) or links the subject to another word in the sentence (linking verb).	Megan *painted* her room. (action) She *felt* pleased with the new color. (linking)
adjective	It modifies a noun or a pronoun.	*green* grass, *two* cats, *that* idea, *your* house, *Mary's* garden
adverb	It modifies a verb, an adjective, or another adverb. Adverbs tell *how, to what extent, when,* or *where*.	Cinderella *quickly scrubbed* the floor. The floor was *very clean*. Cinderella worked *really quickly*.
preposition	It relates a noun or pronoun (its *object*) to some other part of the sentence. An object may be *compound*. The preposition, its object, and any modifiers make up a *prepositional phrase*.	The Jamisons live <u>across</u> the *street*. Sam lent CDs *to <u>Rachel, Henry, and me</u>*. The banner <u>*with green letters*</u> looks best.
conjunction	It connects words or word groups. The coordinating conjunctions are *and, but, or, nor, for,* and *yet*.	*Trophies <u>and</u> ribbons* covered Deena's desk. Wear the scarf *around your neck <u>or</u> across your shoulders*.
interjection	It shows sudden, usually strong, feeling.	*Hey!* Watch where you're going. *Oh*, is that what you think?

In the following passage, underline each common noun <u>once</u> and each proper noun <u>twice</u>. Three items are completed for you as samples. There are 25 more nouns for you to find.

The Metamorphosis is the story of a young salesman named <u>Gregor Samsa</u> who awakens one morning to a shocking discovery: During the night, he has somehow transformed into a giant beetle. One of the first <u>problems</u> he faces is how to get out of bed. He is lying on his back, and he has no idea how to turn over. His numerous little legs stick up into the air and seem to work independently of one another. Finally, Gregor manages to slide onto the <u>floor</u> and drag himself over to the chest of drawers. Using this piece of furniture as a brace, he heaves himself upright.

The rest of this short novel tells how Gregor struggles to make his family understand and accept him in his new manifestation. Franz Kafka, born in Prague in 1883, published the tale in 1915.

ACTIVITY 2

Underline each pronoun. Then draw an arrow from the pronoun to its antecedent.

> **Sample:**
>
> Kelly said <u>she</u> is Gina's understudy.

1. During rehearsals, Yolanda practiced singing her solo.

2. Todd, did you paint the backdrop for the set?

3. The programs are notable for their artsy design.

4. Mrs. Franklin said, "I brought refreshments for the cast."

5. The sofa in center stage should have a spotlight shining on it.

ACTIVITY 3

On each blank, write a pronoun to take the place of the boldfaced antecedent.

> **Sample:**
>
> Did **Margaret** say where __*she*__ was going?

1. The **butterfly** slowly worked _____ way out of the cocoon.

2. **Tomás** uses copper wire and old coins in _____ art.

3. **Class**, have _____ finished Assignment 6 yet?

4. The fresh-baked **rolls** have poppy seeds on _____ .

5. **Betsy** said, "The last piece of peach pie is _____ ."

ACTIVITY 4 _____

Underline the verb in each sentence.

> **Sample:**
>
> Loudly, the gates <u>slammed</u> shut behind us.

1. My little nephew imagined a monster in his closet.

2. In the morning, please make breakfast for everyone.

3. The voice on the telephone sounded cheerful.

4. Finally, the bus arrived at the corner.

5. Maple leaves turn gold in the autumn.

QUESTION: Can a verb consist of more than one word?

ANSWER: Yes. A main verb plus one or more helping verbs is called a *verb phrase.*

VERB PHRASES: Everyone *was laughing* at my joke.

Craig *has been saving* for a dirt bike.

QUESTION: Can a verb include a contraction?

ANSWER: No. To identify the verb, separate the contraction into the words that form it. Then label the words appropriately.

ORIGINAL SENTENCE: I *don't* like beets.

REWRITE AS: I *do not* like beets.

THE VERB: *do like*

(The word *not* is an adverb.)

ACTIVITY 5 _____

Write the verb in each sentence.

> **Sample:**
>
> I'm proofreading my history report right now. _____*am proofreading*_____

1. A mouse has been nibbling at food in the pantry. _____

2. They'll call you for your interview soon. _____

3. I had not realized the depth of her anger. _____

4. Last summer, they'd done everything together. _____

5. These dishes should have been washed. _____

QUESTION: How can I find the verb in a sentence that asks a question?

ANSWER: Rewrite the sentence as a statement. Then identify the verb.

ORIGINAL SENTENCE: Did you get my e-mail?

REWRITE AS: You did get my e-mail.

THE VERB: *Did get*

ACTIVITY 6

Write the verb in each sentence.

Sample:

Haven't you eaten yet? _____*Have eaten*_____

1. Was someone sitting in this chair? _____

2. Were these poems written by T. S. Eliot? _____

3. Can't you stay for one more hour? _____

4. Why were you waiting for me? _____

5. Have you ever felt remorse for a lie? _____

ACTIVITY 7

In the flower below, the five letters in each petal, plus the letter in the middle, can be arranged to spell a verb. Unscramble the six verbs. Then use each verb in a sentence. In your sentences, you can add one or more helping verbs to form a verb phrase.

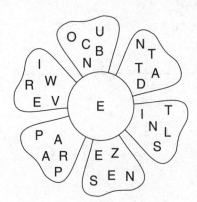

Unscramble Six Verbs

1. _____

2. _____

3. _____

4. _____

5. _____

6. _____

7. _____

8. _____

9. _____

10. _____

11. _____

12. _____

QUESTION: Are the words *the, a,* and *an* adjectives?

ANSWER: Yes. *The, a,* and *an* are a special group of adjectives called *articles.* Since they appear so often, we will exclude them when identifying adjectives in this book.

ACTIVITY 8

Underline each adjective in the following passage. The first two adjectives have been underlined as samples. You should find 22 more adjectives.

A <u>full</u> moon broke through <u>heavy</u> clouds and lit the night. Suddenly, I was illuminated in my lofty position. I stood atop a jumble of boulders at the base of a steep cliff. As legends have it, old Pegleg the pirate stashed a grand treasure somewhere on—or in—this rocky hillside. Over the long years since his untimely death, many have searched for Pegleg's buried wealth. Nobody, however, has found a thing—not one gold doubloon.

However, when lightning struck a tree on this cliff last night, it set off a small avalanche. Now, here I stand on the fallen rocks, staring at a cave that their fall exposed. Back in its dimness, lit only by stray moonbeams, the rich glint of gold winks at me.

Some adjectives are formed from proper nouns and are called *proper adjectives.*

PROPER NOUNS: Shakespeare, America, Brazil

PROPER ADJECTIVES: *Shakespearean* sonnet, *American* flag, *Brazilian* citizen

ACTIVITY 9

Complete each sentence by writing an adjective on the blank.

> **Samples:**
>
> **a.** Toronto is a __Canadian__ city.
>
> **b.** After working in the hot sun, I was __thirsty__ .

1. Your excuse seems _____ .

2. I am an _____ citizen.

3. Yum! This mango tastes _____ .

4. Do you prefer Chinese food or _____ food?

5. At the party, the guests were _____ .

ACTIVITY 10

Underline each adverb in the following sentences. Then draw an arrow to the word it modifies. Some sentences have more than one adverb.

Samples:

a. Is that story really true?

b. Erica is almost never late to class.

1. Kim's coffee was barely warm.

2. The baby awoke too early.

3. Yikes! Ants are crawling everywhere.

4. Quite often, I deposit money in my piggy bank.

5. That stranger's face seems oddly familiar.

6. We will arrive fairly soon.

7. Aunt Becky always seems very happy.

8. Sometimes the roof leaks dreadfully.

9. My test was not scored accurately.

10. The story's conclusion is actually rather tragic.

Study this list of prepositions. Notice that some prepositions, such as *because of*, consist of two words.

about	among	below	despite
above	around	beneath	down
across	as	beside	during
after	at	between	except
against	because of	beyond	for
along	before	but (meaning "except")	from
alongside	behind	by	in

in front of	on	through	up
inside	onto	throughout	upon
in spite of	out	till	with
instead of	out of	to	within
into	outside	toward	without
like	over	under	
of	past	underneath	
off	since	until	

ACTIVITY 11

Underline each preposition <u>once</u> and each object of a preposition <u>twice</u>.

Sample:

Despite <u>warnings</u>, some motorists drove <u>across</u> flooded <u>roads</u>.

1. In the nest rested two eggs with blue shells.

2. Before dawn, my alarm woke me with piercing beeps.

3. The words in that song remind me of an old boyfriend.

4. Throughout the school, teachers and students prepared for final exams.

5. Instead of eggs, grab some waffles out of the freezer.

ACTIVITY 12

Underline each prepositional phrase. Be sure to include all parts of a compound object.

Sample:

<u>Under this dust and grime</u> is a beautiful mirror <u>with a gilt frame</u>.

1. After geometry class, meet me at the soccer field.

2. Within that tough exterior beats the heart of a gentle lamb.

3. Everyone except Juan, Julia, and you were at the pep rally.

4. The forecast is for sleet throughout the evening and night.

5. Out of the slime and muddy weeds crawled a large snapping turtle.

   Note: To find out how to use commas with prepositional phrases, read the Composition Hint on page 79.

Circle the conjunction in each sentence. Then underline each element it connects.

> **Samples:**
>
> **a.** For the fund-raiser, we <u>will organize</u> (and) <u>host</u> a giant rummage sale.
>
> **b.** You can store potatoes *inside the refrigerator* (or) *in a cool, dark cabinet.*

1. Please sweep under the table and behind the sofa.

2. Do you like the stories of Edgar Allan Poe or Nathaniel Hawthorne better?

3. For years, the American artist Georgia O'Keeffe lived and worked in New Mexico.

4. Bessie's new job at the museum is both interesting and challenging.

5. Quietly yet forcefully, I told the child not to touch the snake.

6. Looking for my homework, I searched in my desk and under my bed.

7. My effort to give my friend a makeover was sincere but ineffective.

8. Use black or blue ink to fill out the registration form for pottery class.

9. Fiddling with the radio's dial, I found country, rock, classical, and pop music stations.

10. Deep in the Everglades, the air boat skimmed across a swamp smoothly and quickly.

Composition Hint

When you join items with coordinating conjunctions, make sure the items are of equal rank and structure. That is, join verbs with verbs, not verbs with nouns, and so on.

INSTEAD OF: Wendy is known for her *compassion, kindness,* and *telling good jokes.*

WRITE: Wendy is known for her *compassion, kindness,* and *humor.*

Connecting items of equal rank creates a balance, called *parallel structure,* in your sentence.

Rewrite each sentence to create parallel structure.

> **Samples:**
>
> **a.** The mime moved precisely and with expression.
>
> *The mime moved precisely and expressively.*
>
> **b.** Dedication, perseverance, and being on time are required for the job.
>
> *Dedication, perseverance, and punctuality are required for the job.*

1. School uniforms are convenient but bore me.

   _____

2. Confidently and with skill, Morgan played chess.

   _____

3. Swimming, playing baseball, and to run are my favorite pastimes.

   _____

4. Honesty and a sense of loyalty are crucial in a friend.

   _____

5. I watched Hilda hop, skip, and running down the sidewalk.

   _____

Words commonly used as interjections include the following:

hey	well
hooray	wow
oh	yikes
oops	yuck
ouch	

ACTIVITY 15 _____

What would you say in each of the following situations? Use interjections from the list above to write responses on the lines provided.

Sample:

You catch your little brother looking through your book bag.

Hey! Leave my stuff alone.

1. You pinch your finger while trying to assemble a bicycle.

   _____

2. Your mom tells you to eat the soggy, bland green beans on your plate.

   _____

3. You reluctantly agree to babysit your four younger cousins.

_____

4. You see your best friend shoplift a key chain.

_____

5. You hit a home run in the softball tournament.

_____

2 Review of the Eight Parts of Speech

The eight parts of speech are

- noun
- pronoun
- verb
- adjective
- adverb
- preposition
- conjunction
- interjection

A word's particular role in a sentence determines its part of speech in that sentence.

ACTIVITY 1

On the line provided, write the part of speech of each underlined word or word group.

The Minuet

Mary Mapes Dodge

Grandma told me all <u>about</u> it,   1. _____

Told me so <u>I</u> couldn't doubt it,   2. _____

How she <u>danced</u>, my grandma danced; long ago—   3. _____

How she held her <u>pretty</u> head,   4. _____

How her dainty <u>skirt</u> she spread,   5. _____

How she <u>slowly</u> leaned and rose—long ago.   6. _____

<u>Grandma's</u> hair was bright and sunny,   7. _____

Dimpled cheeks, too, <u>oh</u>, how funny!   8. _____

<u>Really</u> quite a pretty girl—long ago.   9. _____

Bless her! <u>why</u>, she wears a cap,   10. _____

<u>Grandma</u> does, and takes a nap   11. _____

Every single day: <u>and</u> yet   12. _____

Grandma danced the minuet—<u>long</u> ago.   13. _____

"<u>Modern</u> ways are quite alarming,"   14. _____

Grandma says, "<u>but</u> boys were charming"   15. _____

(Girls and boys she means, of course) "long <u>ago</u>." 16. _____

Brave but modest, <u>grandly</u> shy;   17. _____

She <u>would like</u> to have us try   18. _____

Just to feel like <u>those</u> who met   19. _____

<u>In</u> the graceful minuet—long ago.   20. _____

ACTIVITY 2 _____

In "The Minuet" (in Activity 1), the speaker shares fond thoughts of an old person—her grandma. When you think of old people or old age, what ideas and images come to mind? To explore your thoughts, complete Parts I and II below.

Part I

Use the graphic organizer to list nouns, verbs, adjectives, and adverbs that (in your opinion) relate to old age. List **five** words in each category, besides the words written in as samples.

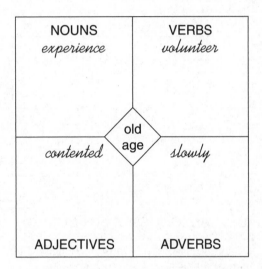

Part II

What do you want your life to be like when you are old? What will you have to do while you are young to achieve this kind of old age? On a separate sheet of paper, write a paragraph answering these questions. Use some or all of the words you listed in the graphic organizer. Use and label all **eight** parts of speech at least once.

ACTIVITY 3 _____

Sort the words in bold type into two lists: nouns and adjectives. Then fit the words into the appropriate puzzle forward, backward, up, or down.

a **winter** day   vanilla **yogurt** for lunch   a loud **school** bell

a red **brick** road   my **orange** vest   notebook **paper**

an **essay** about power   a **college** in Vermont   a **gift** from me

a **bicycle** rack

NOUNS   ADJECTIVES

_____   _____

_____   _____

_____   _____

_____   _____

                    Nouns   Adjectives

Writing Application

Using Nouns as Adjectives

On a separate sheet of paper, list the boldfaced words in Activity 3 that are used as nouns. Then write **five** sentences using each of these nouns as an adjective.

ACTIVITY 4

Decide whether each underlined word is used as a noun or as a verb, and write the part of speech on the short blank. If the word is used as a noun, write a sentence on the long blank using the word as a verb. If it is used as a verb, write a sentence using the word as a noun.

1. a. _____ <u>Quitting</u> is not an option.

   b. _____

2. a. _____ May I see your hall <u>pass</u>, please?

   b. _____

3. a. _____ Do you <u>love</u> me?

    b. _____

4. a. _____ This dry, wilted garden needs <u>rain</u>.

    b. _____

5. a. _____ <u>Shape</u> the clay into a shallow bowl.

    b. _____

ACTIVITY 5

In each sentence below, decide whether the underlined word is used as an adjective or as an adverb. Write the part of speech on the line provided.

1. The most <u>likely</u> winner is Ron Hampton.   _____

2. A security guard checks each room <u>periodically</u>.   _____

3. I love your <u>friendly</u> personality.   _____

4. The <u>early</u> bird catches the worm.   _____

5. May I open my birthday gift <u>early</u>?   _____

ACTIVITY 6

In each sentence below, decide whether the underlined word is used as a preposition or as an adverb, and write the part of speech on the short blank. If the word is used as a preposition, write a sentence on the long blank using the word as an adverb. If it is used as an adverb, write a sentence using the word as a preposition.

1. a. _____ I accidentally left my suitcase <u>behind</u> at the bus station.

    b. _____

2. a. _____ I'll wash all my worries <u>down</u> the drain.

    b. _____

3. a. _____ During the storm, most of the sailors stayed <u>below</u>.

    b. _____

4. a. _____ Is your temper tantrum <u>over</u> now?

    b. _____

5. a. _____ We must finish this lab project <u>before</u> Tuesday.

    b. _____

Parts of Speech

It's time to take a break from traditional grammar exercises. The following activities ask you to explore how people use the eight parts of speech in the real world, outside your class-room walls. Which activity sparks your interest? Choose an activity to complete; then, with your teacher's approval, share the results with your classmates. Have a good time!

Surfers Welcome

Countless students surf the Internet for homework help every day. Create a Web page to serve as a reference source for students who want to learn about the eight parts of speech. Include essential information, such as definitions and examples, and use your design skills to incorporate special fonts, colors, or images. For added credibility, list the sources you consulted for information—your textbook, for example, or a grammar handbook.

Congratulations!

Birthdays, holidays, weddings, births, graduations—what do all these have in common? Greeting cards! Using art supplies or a computer—not to mention your imagination—create one or two original greeting cards. Use each part of speech at least once. On a separate sheet of paper, write the text of each card and label each part of speech.

May Fortune Smile on You

Personification is a literary technique that attributes human actions and char-acteristics to nonhuman things. Compile a list of examples of personification from poems, children's stories, advertisements, books, etc. Which part(s) of speech seem most important to creating personification? Using this information and your imagination, create additional examples of personification (perhaps organized in a list or embedded in a poem or story.)

Shall I Compare Thee to a Summer's Day?

Shakespeare used the eight parts of speech to compose his masterpieces. But have you ever noticed that some of his words are now archaic (old and outdat-ed)? Make a list of archaic words used by Shakespeare and/or other authors. Provide an example of each word in a sentence by the author. Then list the part of speech of the word, along with its modern-day equivalent. In the quotation above (from Shakespeare's sonnet #18) *thee* is a pronoun; its modern-day equivalent is *you*.

Let Me Explain

Which is your favorite part of speech? If you could teach this part of speech to a group of younger students, how would you explain it? Prepare a short lesson on one part of speech, appropriate for students a few years younger than you. Use your own knowledge and ideas, as well as a reliable reference source, to prepare your lesson. Remember to include a definition, examples, and a short activity or exercise to enhance students' learning.

May I Interject?

Often, the interjections we choose say a lot about us. For instance, have you ever exclaimed, "Groovy!"? Perhaps not. How about "Awesome!" or "Rad!"? Do your parents use the same interjections as you do? Prepare a list of interjections that are not printed in Lesson 1. Include interjections that you use, as well as some that you don't use. Then use each interjection in a sentence to illustrate the kind of emotion it conveys.

Parts Department

Investigate the parts of speech of a language besides English and prepare a chart comparing that language to English. Provide examples of each part of speech in each language, taking special note of interjections. Are the same words used as interjections in both languages, or does each have its own interjections? Why do you think this is?

Parts of Speech

Directions: Circle the letter of the best correction for each underlined part and write it on the blank. If the part needs no change, choose the letter for *NO CHANGE*.

_____ 1. Would you like to come over and watch the MTV Movie Awards program <u>television</u>?

    A. NO CHANGE

    B. and television

    C. on television

    D. it

_____ 2. After yelling at my friend, I was <u>real</u> sorry about it and called to apologize.

    F. NO CHANGE

    G. really

    H. reality

    J. Real!

_____ 3. Several students in Mrs. Thompson's math class formed a <u>study</u> group.

    A. NO CHANGE

    B. studious

    C. studiously

    D. studied

_____ 4. The girls' basketball game was <u>competitive riveting</u>.

    F. NO CHANGE

    G. competitive but riveting

    H. competitive or riveting

    J. competitive and riveting

_____ 5. For the Fourth of July, we <u>going</u> to a free concert in Hall Park.

    A. NO CHANGE

    B. be going

    C. are going

    D. is going

_____ 6. Tina and Jeremy took <u>her</u> seat just before the bell rang.

    F. NO CHANGE

    G. his

    H. his or her

    J. their

_____ **7.** <u>Ouch you're</u> stepping on my foot.

    A. NO CHANGE

    B. Ouch, and you're

    C. Ouch, you're

    D. Ouch! You're

_____ **8.** During our trip to Ireland, we marveled at the gorgeous <u>Irish</u> countryside.

    F. NO CHANGE

    G. Irelandish

    H. irish

    J. ireland

_____ **9.** Your performance on the debate team this year has been <u>amazed</u>.

    A. NO CHANGE

    B. amazing

    C. amazingly

    D. amazement

_____ **10.** <u>We</u> going ice skating—would you like to come too?

    F. NO CHANGE

    G. We'll

    H. We're

    J. We's

PART II

Directions: Improve each sentence by rewriting the underlined part using the appropriate part of speech.

11. <u>In a sudden way</u>, my foot skidded on loose rocks, and I fell down.

    _____

12. Margaret Thatcher was the <u>Britain</u> prime minister for three consecutive terms.

    _____

13. I bought a fishbowl, colored gravel, and a <u>fish that was gold</u>.

    _____

14. In 1927, Charles Lindbergh flew <u>Charles Lindbergh's</u> airplane, *The Spirit of St. Louis*, nonstop from New York City to Paris.

    _____

15. During the play, the audience laughed, <u>were crying</u>, and applauded.

    _____

2 Using Grammar and the Mechanics of Writing

We reviewed the parts of speech in Part One. Now, in Part Two, we will focus on grammar and the mechanics of writing. "Mechanics," by the way, simply refers to the technical aspects of writing: punctuation, capitalization, and spelling.

Specifically, Part Two focuses on the *usage* of grammar and mechanics. What is "usage," exactly? We may understand it as the customary, acceptable way that words, phrases, clauses, and mechanics are used in our language. More than simply a matter of language "manners," though, usage is a guide to clear, correct communication.

LESSON

3 Using Verbs

Every complete sentence has at least one verb. When you compose sentences, you must choose the correct tense of the verb and make the verb agree with its subject. In this lesson, you will review and practice these aspects of using verbs in sentences. In addition, you will learn about transitive and intransitive verbs.

Using the Correct Tense

In any kind of writing, formal or informal, we must use the correct *tense* of the verb.

 The *tense* of a verb shows the *time* of the action or the state of being that the verb expresses.

Here are the six main verb tenses, with examples.

PRESENT TENSE: The Statue of Liberty *stands* on Ellis Island.

                         (The action occurs right now, in the present, or is habitually true.)

PAST TENSE: Harriet Tubman *started* the Underground Railroad.

                         (The action occurred in the past.)

FUTURE TENSE: Some baseball cards *will become* valuable over time.

                         (The action will occur at some time in the future.)

PRESENT PERFECT TENSE: Scientists *have placed* a robot on Mars.

                         (The action is completed in the present time. The use of present perfect tense emphasizes the relevance of the action to the current time, right now.)

PAST PERFECT TENSE: By the 1950s, television *had become* an American pastime.

                         (The action was completed before a specific time in the past.)

FUTURE PERFECT TENSE: By 2040, television *will have celebrated* its 100th birthday.

                         (The action will be completed before a specific time in the future.)

Notice that the perfect tenses always use a form of *have (have, has,* or *had).* The future tenses always use *will.*

ACTIVITY 1

Match each underlined verb to its tense. Write the letter of the tense on the line provided. Use each tense only once.

Sample:

___F___ **a.** By Friday, we will have raised over five hundred dollars.

22   Using Grammar and the Mechanics of Writing

_____ **1.** All summer, we <u>hoped</u> for rain.

_____ **2.** My boss <u>has promised</u> me a raise.

_____ **3.** By dinnertime, I <u>had painted</u> my room.

_____ **4.** Each day, Megan <u>eats</u> fruit.

_____ **5.** Warren <u>will call</u> you this weekend.

A. present tense

B. past tense

C. future tense

D. present perfect tense

E. past perfect tense

F̶. future perfect tense

Each of the six verb tenses has a *progressive* form. The progressive form shows that an action or a state of being is ongoing, or continuous. You can recognize the progressive form of a verb by its *ing* ending. Study the examples below.

PRESENT PROGRESSIVE:	Alana *is cooking* dinner right now.
	(The action is continuous in the present.)
PAST PROGRESSIVE:	Alana *was cooking* dinner when you arrived last night.
	(The action was continuous at a time in the past.)
FUTURE PROGRESSIVE:	Alana *will be cooking* dinner between five and six o'clock.
	(The action will be continuous at a time in the future.)
PRESENT PERFECT PROGRESSIVE:	Alana *has been cooking* dinner each night for a week.
	(The action started in the past and is still continuing.)
PAST PERFECT PROGRESSIVE:	For a while, Alana *had been cooking* large, filling dinners.
	(The action was continuous at a time in the past and then ended.)
FUTURE PERFECT PROGRESSIVE:	When August ends, Alana *will have been cooking* dinner nightly for an entire month.
	(The action will be continuous at a time in the future *after* another future action.)

Remember, the perfect tenses always use a form of *have (have, has,* or *had)*. The future tenses always use *will*.

ESL Focus

Using the Present Progressive and the Present Tenses

In English, we use the **present progressive tense** to show that an action or a state of being is happening right now.

PRESENT PROGRESSIVE: I *am reading* a poem.

(The act of reading is occurring right now.)

We use the **present tense** to express an action or a state of being that is always true or that happens habitually (as a habit).

PRESENT TENSE: I *read* poetry. (The act of reading is habitual.)

I *am* Brazilian. (The state of being Brazilian is always true.)

Match each underlined verb to its tense. Write the letter of the tense on the line provided. Use each tense only once.

> **Samples:**
>
> ___C___ **a.** Yolanda <u>will love</u> this ring!
>
> ___D___ **b.** I <u>have</u> definitely <u>found</u> my soul mate.

_____ 1. Yolanda never <u>eats</u> red meat.

_____ 2. Yolanda <u>is eating</u> broccoli with cheese.

_____ 3. When I telephoned, Yolanda <u>was preparing</u> lunch.

_____ 4. She <u>had been planning</u> a simple meal.

_____ 5. I brought over a salad, and we <u>ate</u> together.

_____ 6. Tonight, she and I <u>will be eating</u> together.

_____ 7. We <u>have been planning</u> this evening for weeks.

_____ 8. On the fifteenth, she and I <u>will have been dating</u> for a year.

_____ 9. I <u>had not expected</u> to find a sweetheart at school.

_____ 10. By this time tomorrow, I <u>will have asked</u> Yolanda to marry me.

A. present tense

B. past tense

C̶. future tense

D̶. present perfect tense

E. past perfect tense

F. future perfect tense

G. present progressive

H. past progressive

I. future progressive

J. present perfect progressive

K. past perfect progressive

L. future perfect progressive

Staying With the Same Tense

In your writing, stick with one verb tense unless you have a valid reason for changing tenses.

CONSISTENT TENSE: We *waited* in line and *bought* two tickets.
                   PAST   PAST

MIXED TENSE: We *waited* in line and *buy* two tickets.
                   PAST   PRESENT

QUESTION: How do I recognize mixed verb tense?

ANSWER: To decide whether a sentence has mixed tense, check the tense of each verb. If two or more verbs are in different tenses, you have pinpointed mixed tense.

CONSISTENT TENSE: Reggie *will train* Spike and *will enter* him in the dog show.
                       FUTURE   FUTURE

MIXED TENSE: Reggie *will train* Spike and *entered* him in the dog show.
                   FUTURE   PAST

Underline the verbs in each sentence. Then decide whether the sentence uses consistent tense or mixed tense. On the line provided, write *consistent* or *mixed*.

> **Samples:**
>
> ___mixed___ **a.** We <u>raised</u> the flag and <u>recite</u> the Pledge of Allegiance.
>
> ___consistent___ **b.** The guests <u>have arrived</u> and we <u>have begun</u> the meal.

_____ **1.** On Saturdays, Mr. Adams mows his lawn and trims his hedges.

_____ **2.** Each day, I walk into the cafeteria and looked around for my friends.

_____ **3.** By eight o'clock, I had sold twenty burgers and feel exhausted.

_____ **4.** A snowplow has cleared the streets, and I clear the front walk.

_____ **5.** I will cook dinner if you will wash the dishes.

QUESTION: How do I correct mixed verb tense?

ANSWER: Choose the tense that best expresses the *time* of the action or state of being in the sentence. Rewrite the verb or verbs that are not in this tense.

MIXED TENSE: The team *practiced* faithfully and *wins* most of the games.
                               PAST   PRESENT

CONSISTENT TENSE: The team *practiced* faithfully and *won* most of the games.
                               PAST   PAST

CONSISTENT TENSE: The team *practices* faithfully and *wins* most of the games.
                               PRESENT   PRESENT

Each sentence below has mixed verb tense. Choose the tense that best expresses the time of the action or state of being. Then cross out the incorrect tense and write the correct tense above it.

> **Sample:**
>
>   *scored*
> This morning, Ms. Gray gave us a pop quiz, on which I ~~had scored~~ well.

1. In June, my older brother will go to summer camp, but I stayed home.

2. In their free time, Jessica collected butterflies, and Trina mounts them on pins.

3. By the year 2015, I will have graduated from college and find a great job.

4. Before the fire, many animals live in these meadows and nested in these trees.

5. Before the inspection, employees had cleaned the machinery and test it for accuracy.

Composition Hint

When we write about literature, we use the **present tense**. Why? Every time a person reads a work of literature, the events, characters, and ideas exist *in the present* for that reader. Therefore, we use the present tense—sometimes called the "literary present"—to write and speak about literature.

In *To Kill a Mockingbird,* events <u>take</u> place in a small Alabama town. (NOT *took*)

The author, Harper Lee, <u>tells</u> the story from young Scout's viewpoint. (NOT *told*)

Writing Application — Using Verbs to Write About Literature

Choose a short story that interests you. To find a story, look in an anthology of literature in your classroom or in a library, or ask your teacher for recommendations. Read the short story, paying attention to characters, events, and key ideas.

Using your own words, write two paragraphs summarizing the story's plot. Check your work to make sure you have used the present tense to discuss the work of literature.

Principal Parts of Verbs

In order to use consistent verb tense, we must know the *principal parts of verbs.* The principal parts of a verb are the forms the verb takes in each tense.

A verb has four principal parts. The verb's other forms come from its principal parts.

 The *principal parts* of a verb are the *base form* (*infinitive form*), the *present participle,* the *past,* and the *past participle.*

BASE FORM	PRESENT PARTICIPLE	PAST	PAST PARTICIPLE
laugh	(is) laughing	laughed	(has) laughed

In a sentence, the present participle is always used with a helping verb, such as *is.* For this reason, in the present participle column above, *is* appears in parentheses before the verb form. Similarly, the past participle is always used with the helping verb *has, have,* or *had.* Therefore, we place *has* in parentheses before the past participle form.

ACTIVITY 5

Complete the table below by filling in the missing parts of each verb.

	BASE FORM	PRESENT PARTICIPLE	PAST	PAST PARTICIPLE
1.	bake	(is) _____	baked	(has) _____
2.	_____	(is) paying	_____	(has) paid
3.	paint	(is) _____	_____	(has) painted
4.	_____	(is) fixing	fixed	(has) _____
5.	practice	(is) practicing	_____	(has) _____

Regular Verbs

Most verbs are *regular.* They form tenses (that is, they express time of an action) in regular, predictable ways.

 A *regular verb* forms the past and past participle by adding *d* or *ed* to the base form.

Here are examples of the principal parts of some regular verbs.

BASE FORM	PRESENT PARTICIPLE	PAST	PAST PARTICIPLE
clap	(is) clapping	clapped	(has) clapped
jump	(is) jumping	jumped	(has) jumped
kick	(is) kicking	kicked	(has) kicked
shop	(is) shopping	shopped	(has) shopped
comb	(is) combing	combed	(has) combed

ACTIVITY 6

Write sentences that follow the directions below.

> **Sample:**
>
> Use the past participle of *look.*
>
> _____ The brothers have looked everywhere for an affordable scooter. _____

1. Use the past tense of *ask.*

_____

2. Use the past participle of *seem.*

_____

3. Use the present participle of *lock*.

_____

4. Use the base form of *shout*.

_____

5. Use the past participle of *e-mail*.

_____

Irregular Verbs

Some verbs do not form their past and past participle forms in the regular way.

 An *irregular verb* <u>does not</u> form the past and past participle by adding *d* or *ed* to the base form.

For example, the verb *write* is irregular. To form the past tense of *write,* we do not add *d* to form *writed*. Instead, we respell the word as *wrote*. The past participle takes another spelling: *written*.

Another irregular verb is *freeze*. The past tense is *froze* (not *freezed*), and the past participle is *frozen* (not *freezed* or *frozed*).

ACTIVITY 7 _____

Two verbs are spelled backward in each line of the puzzle. Circle each verb, then write it in the appropriate column: Regular Verbs or Irregular Verbs.

Regular Verbs   Irregular Verbs

1. _____ I D N I F H T R E L G G U J U D H A Y P _____
2. _____ S U W O R H T E Q V A M R Y Y A L P G S _____
3. _____ V K N I R D P E T S K U I B N H G K I O _____
4. _____ D E S F Q Y U K C P O O C S Z M I W S L _____
5. _____ Y R R A M J O E V I R D L B Q V H U U F _____
6. _____ I A K A E R B X J C A A S S O T R W R P _____
7. _____ Z H I D P O O N W F K N I L B E V A E L _____
8. _____ N G H C A X H C R A M E K N I H T L H C _____
9. _____ Y R E H C T A C T V K Y B I P O T S U I _____
10. _____ O W W O N K N D F L L E M S U M B O D T _____

QUESTION: What is the rule for forming the principal parts of irregular verbs?

ANSWER: There is no single rule for forming the principal parts of irregular verbs. Instead, each word has its own peculiar forms. To use irregular verbs correctly, we must learn their forms.

Here is a list of the trickiest irregular verbs. Read over the list until you become familiar with the correct forms of the principal parts. Moreover, refer to this list whenever you have a question about the principal parts of one of these verbs.

PRINCIPAL PARTS OF 40 IRREGULAR VERBS

BASE FORM	PRESENT PARTICIPLE	PAST	PAST PARTICIPLE
become	(is) becoming	became	(has) become
begin	(is) beginning	began	(has) begun
blow	(is) blowing	blew	(has) blown
break	(is) breaking	broke	(has) broken
bring	(is) bringing	brought	(has) brought
catch	(is) catching	caught	(has) caught
choose	(is) choosing	chose	(has) chosen
come	(is) coming	came	(has) come
do	(is) doing	did	(has) done
draw	(is) drawing	drew	(has) drawn
drink	(is) drinking	drank	(has) drunk
drive	(is) driving	drove	(has) driven
eat	(is) eating	ate	(has) eaten
fall	(is) falling	fell	(has) fallen
find	(is) finding	found	(has) found
fly	(is) flying	flew	(has) flown
freeze	(is) freezing	froze	(has) frozen
get	(is) getting	got	(has) gotten *or* got
give	(is) giving	gave	(has) given
go	(is) going	went	(has) gone
hold	(is) holding	held	(has) held
know	(is) knowing	knew	(has) known
lay	(is) laying	laid	(has) laid
lie	(is) lying	lay	(has) lain
ride	(is) riding	rode	(has) ridden
rise	(is) rising	rose	(has) risen
say	(is) saying	said	(has) said
see	(is) seeing	saw	(has) seen
shake	(is) shaking	shook	(has) shaken
sit	(is) sitting	sat	(has) sat
speak	(is) speaking	spoke	(has) spoken
stick	(is) sticking	stuck	(has) stuck
swim	(is) swimming	swam	(has) swum
take	(is) taking	took	(has) taken
teach	(is) teaching	taught	(has) taught
tear	(is) tearing	tore	(has) torn
throw	(is) throwing	threw	(has) thrown
win	(is) winning	won	(has) won
wind	(is) winding	wound	(has) wound
write	(is) writing	wrote	(has) written

ACTIVITY 8

In each sentence, underline the correct form of the verb.

> **Sample:**
>
> Two red helium balloons (*rised*, <u>*rose*</u>) into the sky.

1. Tyrell has (*rode, ridden*) his bicycle to his best friend's house.

2. Impulsively, Sharla (*bought, buyed*) a stack of magazines.

3. Darryl claims that he (*caught, catched*) a foot-long catfish.

4. At the party, thirsty guests (*drunk, drank*) every last drop of the punch.

5. Unfortunately, these shoes have (*lain, lied*) outside in the rain all night.

ACTIVITY 9

On the blank, write the correct form of the verb in parentheses.

> **Sample:**
>
> Grinning, Josh _____*shook*_____ the gift to see if it rattled.
> (*past tense of <u>shake</u>*)

1. Fritz _____ an action-packed poem about basketball. (*past tense of <u>write</u>*)

2. Hurricane winds have _____ down telephone lines. (*past participle form of <u>blow</u>*)

3. Ouch! I accidentally _____ my finger with a tack. (*past tense of <u>stick</u>*)

4. Grandma has _____ that clock daily for ten years. (*past participle form of <u>wind</u>*)

5. Hungrily, the girls _____ hamburgers and fries. (*past tense of <u>eat</u>*)

 Writing
Application   Using Irregular Verbs

On a separate sheet of paper, write **five** sentences, each one using the **past tense** of an irregular verb. Then, with your teacher's approval, exchange papers with a classmate. Now, write **five** more sentences, this time using the **past participle** forms of the verbs in your classmate's sentences. Share the results with your classmate.

Agreement of Subject and Verb

In a sentence, a verb must agree with its subject in *number*. That is, if the subject of a sentence is singular, the verb must also be singular. If the subject is plural, the verb must also be plural.

	SINGULAR	PLURAL
Nouns:	Todd runs	athletes run
Pronouns:		
First Person:	I run	we run
Second Person:	you run	you run
Third Person:	he, she, it runs	they run

ACTIVITY 10

Underline the correct form of the verb in parentheses.

> **Samples:**
>
> **a.** Pam (*sleeps*, sleep) nine hours every night.
>
> **b.** On the bus, we (prefers, *prefer*) the back seats.

1. I (*believes, believe*) in the importance of selfless acts of kindness.

2. During a full moon, the dogs (*howls, howl*) eerily.

3. This faucet (*leaks, leak*) about a gallon of water a day.

4. You (*enjoys, enjoy*) baseball, right?

5. Each year, we (*plans, plan*) the spring formal with great care and flair.

The verb *to be,* the most common verb in English, is irregular. As a result, it poses special challenges to writers. Take a look at the present and past tenses of *to be:*

	PRESENT TENSE		PAST TENSE	
	SINGULAR	PLURAL	SINGULAR	PLURAL
First Person	I am	we are	I was	we were
Second Person	you are	you are	you were	you were
Third Person	he, she, it is	they are	he, she, it was	they were

Another important yet challenging verb is *to have.* Take a look at its present and past tenses.

	PRESENT TENSE		PAST TENSE	
	SINGULAR	PLURAL	SINGULAR	PLURAL
First Person	I have	we have	I had	we had
Second Person	you have	you have	you had	you had
Third Person	he, she, it has	they have	he, she, it had	they had

Write sentences that follow the directions below.

> **Sample:**
>
> Use the subject *friends* and the past tense of *to be*.
>
> My friends were on the honor roll last semester.

1. Use the subject *I* and the present tense of *to be*.

_____

2. Use the subject *you* and the present tense of *to have*.

_____

3. Use the subject *Harriet* and the present tense of *to have*.

_____

4. Use the subject *teachers* and the present tense of *to be*.

_____

5. Use the subject *dog* and the past tense of *to be*.

_____

Most native speakers of English tend to use the right form of a verb when it immediately follows the subject in a sentence. Here is an example:

A <u>bird</u> <u>nibbles</u> birdseed from the feeder.

In other sentences, subject-verb agreement is not as simple, and mistakes commonly occur. Study the following guidelines for subject-verb agreement.

1. Words that come between the subject and the verb do not affect subject-verb agreement.

The *surfboard* with blue stripes *is* mine.

2. Expressions such as *with, together with, according to, including, as well as, plus,* and *no less than* do not affect subject-verb agreement.

A *lawyer*, together with two paralegals, *has entered* the elevator.

(Remember, only a conjunction such as *and* can join two words to form a compound subject. *Together with* is not a conjunction.)

3. The conjunctions *and, or, nor, either . . . or,* and *neither . . . nor* signal the presence of a compound subject.

(a) When subjects are connected by *and,* the subject is plural and the verb is usually plural.

A <u>paralegal</u> *and* a <u>lawyer</u> <u>have entered</u> the elevator.

(The conjunction *and* joins the singular *paralegal* to the singular *lawyer* to form a compound subject. The subject as a whole refers to two people, so it is considered a plural subject.)

A <u>paralegal</u> *and* two <u>lawyers</u> <u>have entered</u> the elevator.

(In this compound subject, the conjunction *and* signals a joining of ideas (*paralegal and lawyers*). The subject as a whole refers to three people, so it is considered a plural subject.)

(b) When subjects are joined by *or, nor, either . . . or,* or *neither . . . nor,* the verb agrees with the nearer subject.

An <u>apple</u> *or* two <u>plums</u> <u>are</u> in each child's snack pack.

(In this compound subject, the conjunction *or* signals the *separation* of ideas (*apple or plums*). The subject as a whole refers to *either* an apple *or* plums, but *not* an apple and plums. Therefore, the verb agrees with whichever part of the compound subject is closer to it. Since the plural noun *plums* is closer to the verb, the verb is plural.)

Two <u>plums</u> *or* an <u>apple</u> <u>is</u> in each child's snack pack.

(This compound subject has parts in the reverse order as those in the example above. As you can see, *apple* is now closer to the verb. Since *apple* is singular, the verb is singular.)

Either the <u>dog</u> *or* the <u>cats</u> <u>have made</u> this mess.

(Just like the conjunction *or,* the conjunction *either . . . or* signals a separation of ideas. In this example, either the dog has made the mess or the cats have made the mess—but NOT the dog *and* the cats. It's one or the other, and the verb agrees with whichever one is nearer it. In this case, the plural *cats* is nearer, so the verb is plural.)

Neither the <u>cats</u> *nor* the <u>dog</u> <u>has made</u> this mess.

(Just like *either . . . or,* the conjunction *neither . . . nor* signals the separation of ideas. In this case, the singular *dog* is nearer the verb, so the verb is singular.)

4. *You* always takes a plural verb.

Dana, <u>you</u> <u>are</u> in charge. (NOT *you is*)

Dana and Cassidy, <u>you</u> <u>are</u> in charge.

5. When the subject follows the verb, find the subject and make the verb agree with it.

<u>Was</u> the <u>bridge</u> over Miller's Crossing safe? (*singular subject and singular verb*)

Here <u>are</u> the <u>reports</u> on the managers' expenses. (*plural subject and plural verb*)

Near the park's entrance <u>stands</u> a giant carved <u>bear</u>. (*singular subject and singular verb*)

In each sentence, underline the subject and the correct form of the verb in parentheses. Be sure to underline all parts of a compound subject, but not words that come between the subject and verb.

Samples:

a. The <u>exhibit</u> of reptiles in their natural habitats (<u>*is*</u>, *are*) over here.

b. Today, the <u>newspaper</u> and the <u>radio</u> (*is*, <u>*are*</u>) featuring stories on local heroes.

1. Neither Donnie nor his friends (*likes, like*) opera music.

2. From farms large and small (*comes, come*) food for America.

3. One egg or two egg whites (*is, are*) included in this muffin recipe.

4. Frida, you (*was, were*) supposed to meet me an hour ago.

5. Three plump hens and a red rooster (*lives, live*) in this coop.

6. My cousin, plus all her suitcases, (*was, were*) waiting at the baggage-claim area.

7. Neither the students nor the teacher (*wants, want*) a longer school year.

8. Neither the teacher nor the students (*wants, want*) a longer school year.

9. The painting, including its lovely frame, (*costs, cost*) a hundred dollars.

10. Only one person in thousands (*wins, win*) the grand prize.

Five Troublesome Verb Pairs

Some verb pairs cause more than their share of problems. Learn the correct use of each verb in the following pairs. (Some of these words may be used as one or more parts of speech in addition to the verb, but here we will focus on their uses as verbs.)

First, study the definitions of the words and examples of their usage. Then look at the table that follows to see the principal parts of each verb.

Accept, Except

accept: to receive willingly. *I accept your offer.*

except: to leave out, to exclude. *The manager excepted all designer labels from the semi-annual sale.*

Affect, Effect

affect: to influence. *Did the rain affect the tournament yesterday?*

effect: to accomplish or bring about. *The principal's warning effected a change in Tory's behavior.*

Bring, Take

bring: to carry or lead, usually toward the speaker. *Please bring your history notes to my house.*

take: to get something into one's possession; to grasp; to carry away. *Please take my hand, and we will take this gift to our neighbor.*

Lie, Lay

lie: to rest or recline. *May I lie on your sofa?*

lay: to put or set something down. *Please lay this blanket on the sofa.*

Sit, Set

sit: to occupy a chair. *Let's sit in the front row.*

set: to place or put something somewhere. *You can set your tub of popcorn on the armrest.*

PRINCIPAL PARTS OF TROUBLESOME VERBS

BASE FORM	PRESENT PARTICIPLE	PAST	PAST PARTICIPLE
accept	(is) accepting	accepted	(has) accepted
affect	(is) affecting	affected	(has) affected
bring	(is) bringing	brought	(has) brought
effect	(is) effecting	effected	(has) effected
except	(is) excepting	excepted	(has) excepted
lay	(is) laying	laid	(has) laid
lie	(is) lying	lay	(has) lain
set	(is) setting	set	(has) set
sit	(is) sitting	sat	(has) sat
take	(is) taking	took	(has) taken

ACTIVITY 13 _____

Write the correct verb in parentheses on the blank in the sentence.

> **Sample:**
>
> Janet found a wallet _____lying_____ on the sidewalk. (*laying, lying*)

1. Did your father _____ the job offer in Chicago? (*accept, except*)

2. We can _____ this small rug over the stain in the carpet. (*lay, lie*)

3. Candace, will you _____ this package to the post office and mail it? (*bring, take*)

4. An employee was _____ new merchandise in the front window. (*setting, sitting*)

5. I believe that recycling can _____ a change in the environment. (*affect, effect*)

6. Residents outside the state of Virginia are _____ from this offer. (*accepted, excepted*)

7. Janeese and her friends _____ in the sun by the swimming pool. (*laid, lay*)

8. The candidate's campaign promises _____ my opinion of her. (*affected, effected*)

9. When you come to my house, please _____ potato chips or soda with you. (*bring, take*)

10. That broken-down car has _____ in the neighbors' driveway for months. (*set, sat*)

Writing Application

Using Troublesome Verbs

On a separate sheet of paper, write **five** sentences, each one using the **past tense** of a troublesome verb. Then, with your teacher's approval, exchange papers with a classmate. Now, write **five** more sentences, this time using the **past participle** forms of the verbs in your classmate's sentences. Share the results with your classmate.

Transitive and Intransitive Verbs

In both sentences below, the verb is *ate.* What is the difference in how the verb is used?

1. Victor *ate.*

2. Victor *ate* the taco.

In sentence 1, *ate* expresses action, and that is all. We say that this verb is *intransitive.* In sentence 2, *ate* expresses action upon a direct object, *taco.* We say that this verb is *transitive.*

 An *intransitive verb* is a linking verb or an action verb that does *not* take an object.

 A *transitive verb* is an action verb that takes an object.

INTRANSITIVE: Everyone *relaxed.* (action verb)

Tessa *is studying* diligently. (action verb)

Doug *felt* thankful. (linking verb)

TRANSITIVE: Tessa *studied* calculus diligently. (*Calculus* is a direct object.)

Phina *wrote* a letter. (*Letter* is a direct object.)

Phina *has written* Oscar a letter. (*Letter* is a direct object; *Oscar* is an indirect object.)

ACTIVITY 14 _____

Underline the verb in each sentence. Then, on the line provided, tell how it is used. Write *I* for *intransitive* or *T* for *transitive*.

> **Samples:**
>
> ___I___ **a.** An up-and-coming star in the film world <u>is</u> M. Night Shyalaman.
>
> ___T___ **b.** He <u>has been making</u> movies since childhood.

_____ **1.** Shyalaman is famous for films such as *Unbreakable* and *Signs.*

_____ **2.** During high school, Shyalaman earned scholarships to medical school.

_____ **3.** However, his true dream was film school.

_____ **4.** In New York, he attended the NYU Tisch School of the Arts.

_____ **5.** There, he honed his skills as a writer, an actor, and a director.

_____ **6.** His first big hit was *The Sixth Sense.*

_____ **7.** The film received six Academy Award nominations.

_____ **8.** In this thriller, Bruce Willis portrays a psychologist.

_____ **9.** Besides Willis, Shyalaman has worked with other stars, including Rosie O'Donnell, Denis Leary, Samuel L. Jackson, and Mel Gibson.

_____ **10.** In 2004, Shyalaman released *The Village* to much fanfare.

You may have noticed that some action verbs may be either transitive or intransitive. It depends on how they are used in the sentence.

INTRANSITIVE: Trevor *hummed* happily. (no object)

TRANSITIVE: Trevor *hummed* a tune happily. (*Tune* is a direct object.)

A linking verb is always intransitive. However, some verbs can be used as either a linking verb or an action verb, so you have to look at how the verb is used in the sentence.

INTRANSITIVE: Bastién *grows* taller every day. (no object)

TRANSITIVE: Bastién *grows* herbs in his garden. (*Herbs* is a direct object.)

Here are a few verbs that may be used either as action verbs or linking verbs:

feel, grow, smell, sound, taste, turn

On the lines below, write five sentences using intransitive verbs and five sentences using transitive verbs. Choose your verbs from the following list. Not all words in the list will be used.

taste   dance   play   memorize   turn   plan   review
whisper   jiggle   believe freeze   smell   repair   sleep

Intransitive Verbs

Sample:

Gigi has been planning for a vacation in San Diego.

1. _____
2. _____
3. _____
4. _____
5. _____

Transitive Verbs

Sample:

Do you believe me?

6. _____
7. _____
8. _____
9. _____
10. _____

4 Using Nouns

As you recall from Lesson 1, a *noun* is a word that names a person, place, thing, animal, or idea. In this lesson, we will review different types of nouns and how they are used in sentences.

Concrete Nouns and Abstract Nouns

Most nouns fall clearly into one of two categories: concrete or abstract.

 A *concrete noun* names a person, place, animal, or thing that can be perceived with at least one of the five senses (sight, smell, taste, touch, hearing).

<u>Aladdin</u> rubbed the <u>lamp</u>, and a <u>genie</u> appeared. (concrete nouns)

 An *abstract noun* names a quality, feeling, or idea. It cannot be perceived by any of the five senses.

To Aladdin's <u>delight</u>, he received three <u>wishes</u>. (abstract nouns)

ACTIVITY 1 _____

Decide whether each noun in the following list is concrete or abstract. Then, in the appropriate section, use the noun in a sentence.

loyalty	announcement	music	smoke	contentment	salt
solitude	concentration	justice	elevator	distance	moon

Concrete Nouns

Sample:

<u>We listened to a brief announcement from our principal.</u>

1. _____

2. _____

3. _____

4. _____

5. _____

Abstract Nouns

6. _____

7. _____

8. _____

9. _____

10. _____

Collective Nouns

You can think of a collective noun as a word that refers to a collection of individual things. These things may be people, animals, or objects. For example, *audience* is a collective noun that names a group of people. *Herd* names a group of animals.

 A *collective noun* names a group of individual things as a unit.

Here is a list of collective nouns.

audience	crowd	number	swarm
batch	flock	orchestra	team
bunch	gaggle	pride	
cluster	jury	set	
committee	litter	staff	

QUESTION: Is a collective noun considered singular or plural?

ANSWER: It usually depends on how the noun is used in the sentence. Follow these two guidelines:

(a) If the sentence is speaking about the group *as a whole,* the collective noun is singular. Use a **singular verb** or **singular pronoun** in reference to it.

The <u>herd</u> of cows <u>prefers</u> grain to hay.

(This sentence says something about the group of animals as a unit—as one thing. Remember, words coming between the subject and verb do not affect subject-verb agreement.)

The <u>audience</u> rose to *its* feet.

(This sentence says something about the group of people as a unit—as one thing.)

(b) If the sentence is speaking about the *individual things* in the group, the collective noun is plural. Use a **plural verb** or **plural pronoun** in reference to it.

The <u>audience</u> were milling around the lobby and in the aisles.

(This sentence refers to the group of people as individuals—as many things.)

The <u>herd</u> are protective of ***their*** calves.

(This sentence refers to the group of animals as individuals.)

ACTIVITY 2

In each sentence, underline the collective noun. Then underline the word in parentheses that agrees with the noun.

> **Samples:**
>
> **a.** In the jungle, a <u>pride</u> of lions (*<u>was</u>, were*) lounging in warm sunlight.
>
> **b.** A <u>number</u> of respondents expressed (*its, <u>their</u>*) opinions at length.

1. The batch of cookies (*has, have*) been tucked into our lunches or stored in the cookie jar.

2. During each trial, the jury (*sits, sit*) in these chairs.

3. On Friday, the committee will hold (*its, their*) monthly meeting.

4. This litter of kittens (*is, are*) being adopted by several different families.

5. A bunch of us (*is, are*) eating at picnic tables, on park benches, or in cars.

6. The crowd (*belongs, belong*) behind the yellow line at all times.

7. The team tried (*its, their*) best, but the opponents were victorious.

8. Until recently, the set of dishes (*was, were*) displayed in this china hutch.

9. A flock of sparrows (*rests, rest*) in the trees and shrubs near the lily pond.

10. Did the staff turn in (*its, their*) activity sheets for approval?

Writing Application

Using Collective Nouns

On a separate sheet of paper, write **ten** sentences using the collective nouns in Activity 2. If the noun was used as a singular noun in the activity, use it as a plural noun in your sentence. If it was used as a plural noun, use it as a singular noun in your sentence.

Count and Noncount Nouns

The difference between count and noncount nouns is the quality of being countable.

 A *count noun* names something that can be counted.

COUNT NOUNS: pencil, friend, hat, sandwich, key, cloud, fingernail

Count nouns exist as separate units and are therefore countable. *One pencil, two friends, several hats*. As you can see, these nouns have a singular form and a plural form.
Count nouns usually (but not always) name concrete nouns—that is, things that we can perceive with our senses.

 A *noncount noun* names something that cannot be counted.

NONCOUNT NOUNS: furniture, respect, rice, air, water, homework, education

A noncount noun usually names a whole that we don't think of as countable. As a result, these nouns usually do not have a plural form.

Where should I deliver the *furniture?* (NOT furnitures)

How much homework do you have? (NOT How many homeworks)

ACTIVITY 3

Sort the nouns into the appropriate columns—count or noncount.

| weather | oxygen | idea | nature | envelope | stripe |
| shoe | English | information | year | ice | warning |

(weather and shoe are crossed out)

Samples:

COUNT NOUNS	NONCOUNT NOUNS
a. _____shoe_____	b. _____weather_____

1. _____   6. _____

2. _____   7. _____

3. _____   8. _____

4. _____   9. _____

5. _____   10. _____

Using Articles with Count and Noncount Nouns

As you recall, the words *a, an,* and *the* are a special group of adjectives called *articles*. These words are used before nouns and pronouns.

a pencil   *an* apple   *the* rice

We use *the* with count and noncount nouns to indicate a specific item.

Please hand me *the pencil.* (one specific pencil)

Did you like *the rice*? (a specific dish of rice)

When a count noun is singular and indefinite, we use *a* or *an* before it.

Please hand me *a pencil.* (any pencil at all)

Would you like *an apple*? (any apple at all)

We do not usually use *a* or *an* with noncount nouns. Often, however, we use the adjective *some*.

Ahmad ate *rice* and a steak. (NOT *a rice*)

Ahmad ate *some rice* and a steak.

To express quantities of noncount nouns, we generally use units of measure.

Ahmad bought *a quart* of milk. (but NOT *a milk*)

Ahmed bought *a loaf* of bread. (but NOT *a bread*)

Ahmed bought *some loaves* of bread.

Ahmed bought *three loaves* of bread. (but NOT *some three loaves*)

ACTIVITY 4

On each blank, write *a, an, the,* or *some,* as appropriate. Then, on the blank at the end of the sentence, state whether the noun in boldface is count or noncount.

Samples:

a. Who is responsible for __the__ **graffiti** on this wall? __noncount__

b. For English class, Seth wrote __a__ **poem.** __count__

COUNT OR NONCOUNT?

1. Would you like _____ **broccoli**? _____

2. Please move _____ **chair** so I can mop the floor. _____

3. At the market, Freddie selected _____ **pineapple**. _____

4. There is _____ **mail** on the hall table for you. _____

5. Amira lives in _____ **apartment** near school. _____

6. _____ **bee** stung me on the arm.   _____

7. Who left _____ **milk** sitting out all night?   _____

8. Ana made _____ **jewelry** in this case by hand.   _____

9. You may complete _____ **assignment** with a partner. _____

10. Dimitri posted _____ **poetry** on the Web.   _____

ACTIVITY 5 _____

In Part I, place each letter in the box in the grid below to form a noun of five or more letters, reading left to right. Compound nouns and plural nouns are not used. Two nouns are completed as samples. Instructions for Part II follow the puzzle.

Part I

| Y | N | R | X | C | O | A | S | D | E | T | X |

Samples: **a.**

M	J	U	Q	I	B	G	A	G	G	L	E	Z
R	Y	W	U	C	O	u	R	A	G	E	A	N
E	I	N	G	R	E		I	E	N	T	R	E
V	A	C	A	T	I		N	A	P	T	H	C
T	U	M	E	R	C		C	K	O	O	D	Y
A	Q	S	C	L	U		T	E	R	L	O	P
P	Y	E	I	D	M		C	H	A	N	I	C
U	I	M	A	G	I		A	T	I	O	N	N
R	S	O	S	W	A		M	F	U	P	C	V
M	A	B	A	G	G		G	E	O	X	B	I
O	V	G	G	O	R		H	E	S	T	R	A
T	E	H	C	L	O		H	I	N	G	I	L

(rows labeled b., 1., 2., 3., 4., 5., 6., 7., 8., 9., 10.)

Part II

On the numbered line corresponding to each line of the puzzle, write the noun you found in that line. Then write whether the noun is *concrete* or *abstract,* whether it is *count* or *noncount,* and whether it collective (*yes* or *no*).

Samples:

	NOUN	CONCRETE OR ABSTRACT?	COUNT OR NONCOUNT?	COLLECTIVE?
a.	gaggle	concrete	count	yes
b.	courage	abstract	noncount	no

NOUN	CONCRETE OR ABSTRACT?	COUNT OR NONCOUNT?	COLLECTIVE?
1. _____	_____	_____	_____
2. _____	_____	_____	_____
3. _____	_____	_____	_____
4. _____	_____	_____	_____
5. _____	_____	_____	_____
6. _____	_____	_____	_____
7. _____	_____	_____	_____
8. _____	_____	_____	_____
9. _____	_____	_____	_____
10. _____	_____	_____	_____

5 Using Modifiers

The job of a modifier is to make the meaning of a word in the sentence more clear or exact. This lesson focuses on modifiers that consist of one word. Later in this book, Lessons 12 and 13 give information about modifiers that take the form of a phrase. Lesson 14 gives information on modifiers that take the form of a clause.

The main thing to remember is that, no matter what form the modifier takes, there are only two kinds of modifiers: adjectives and adverbs. As you recall from Lesson 1, an *adjective* modifies a noun or a pronoun. An *adverb* modifies a verb, an adjective, or an adverb.

QUESTION: Why do we use modifiers?

ANSWER: Modifiers enhance a sentence's basic expression of thought by adding exactness and clarity. Notice the difference modifiers make in these examples:

1. Doves flew.

2. One hundred white doves flew gracefully upward.

3. Frantically, two doves flew crazily upward.

The bare sentence in 1 is made more vivid by the added modifiers in sentence 2. *One hundred, white, gracefully,* and *upward* create a mental image of beauty and grace. In contrast, the modifiers in sentence 3—*Frantically, two, crazily, upward*—create a mental image of panic and chaos.

ACTIVITY 1

Add exactness and clarity to each sentence by adding modifiers. Write your new sentences on the lines provided.

> **Sample:**
>
> Students talked.
>
> _____Several new students talked shyly yet sociably._____

1. Darnell worked on the project.

   _____

2. Musicians performed.

   _____

3. People dislike weather.

   _____

4. We arrived.

_____

5. Smells filled the shop.

_____

Articles, Demonstratives, and Quantifiers

Articles, demonstratives, and _quantifiers_ are three specific types of adjectives. Like all adjectives, they are used to modify nouns and pronouns in sentences.

TYPES OF ADJECTIVE	HOW TO USE THEM	EXAMPLES
The **articles** are _a, an,_ and _the._	(a) Use _a_ and _an_ before general, singular nouns and to indicate _one._ (b) Use _the_ before specific nouns and noncount nouns. (c) Use _the_ before an ordinal number or a superlative.	(a) _An_ airplane flew overhead and cast _a_ shadow. (b) _The_ air smelled fresh after _the_ rainstorm. (c) _The_ third question was _the_ hardest one.
The **demonstratives** are _this, that, these,_ and _those._	Use them to point out a specific noun.	Do you want _this_ apple? _That_ joke was an old one. Trey made _these_ clay pots. Please box _those_ things for storage.
Quantifiers modify nouns by indicating a general quantity.	Use them to indicate a general quantity. Common quantifiers are _a little, a lot of, any, enough, few, many, most, much, several,_ and _some._	Please wait a _few_ minutes. Do you want _some_ pie? I don't have _any_ money. I need _a little_ time to think.

ACTIVITY 2 _____

Fill in each blank with one of the adjectives given as a choice.

> **Samples:**
>
> In the following sentences, fill in the blanks with _a, this, the,_ or _enough._
>
> **a.** Does Franka have _____enough_____ time to retype the essay?
>
> **b.** When I got to _____the_____ corner, I realized I had left my wallet at home.

1. In the following sentences, fill in the blanks with _a, an,_ or _the._

a. Shaniqua is saving up to buy _____ ten-speed bike.

b. This is _____ fifth e-mail that Scott has sent me.

_____

c. Your accountant made _____ error in her bookkeeping.

d. Isn't _____ weather beautiful today?

2. In the following sentences, fill in the blanks with *this, that, these,* or *those.*

   a. For your report, you may choose from among _____ topics.

   b. Wow! _____ flower is gorgeous.

   c. Where did you get _____ flowers you are carrying?

   d. Please take _____ basket of fruit to Mrs. Waverly next door.

3. In the following sentences, fill in the blanks with *a little, a lot of, any, enough, few, many, most, much, several,* or *some.*

   a. No, thank you. I don't want _____ dessert tonight.

   b. By midnight, _____ cars were still parked outside the theater.

   c. _____ people I know are honest, kind, and hardworking.

   d. We cannot afford _____ more of these expensive restaurant meals.

   e. Georgia needs to find _____ books on underwater volcanoes.

   f. This poor dog has _____ fleas in his fur.

   g. The box will not hold _____ more.

All the demonstratives and many of the quantifiers may be used either as an adjective or as a pronoun.

ADJECTIVE:	Who wrote *this* note?
PRONOUN:	Who wrote *this*?
ADJECTIVE:	*Most* students passed the exam.
PRONOUN:	*Most* passed the exam.
ADJECTIVE:	I don't own *any* skis.
PRONOUN:	I don't own *any*.

Writing Application   **Using Demonstratives and Quantifiers**

Choose **five** demonstratives and quantifiers from the table on page 47. On a separate sheet of paper, write **ten** sentences. In five sentences, use the modifiers as adjectives. In the other five sentences, use the modifiers as pronouns. (You can write the sentences in any order.) Underline the modifier in each sentence.

   With your teacher's approval, exchange sentences with a classmate. Label the use of each demonstrative and quantifier in your classmate's sentences and then share the results with each other.

Articles

Not every noun in a sentence needs an article before it. You should omit (leave out) the article
- when you are using a demonstrative: May I borrow *that* pencil?
- before a general noncount noun: Alma will eat *oatmeal*.
- before a general plural noun: Mika likes *kittens*.
- before names of days of the week: Ramiro arrived on *Monday*.

In addition, certain common expressions omit articles:

go to bed   go to class   go to college   go to school   go to church

ACTIVITY 3

Decide whether the underlined article in each sentence is needed. If it is needed, write *C* for *correct* on the blank. If it is not needed, cross it out.

Samples:

___*C*___ **a.** Did you buy <u>the</u> supplies we need?

_____ **b.** This store sells t~~he~~ supplies for artists.

_____ **1.** I need to go to <u>the</u> class now, but I'll see you later.

_____ **2.** Julio likes <u>the</u> mangoes, but he doesn't have any in his refrigerator.

_____ **3.** What is <u>the</u> secret ingredient in your recipe for enchiladas?

_____ **4.** Let's get together on <u>the</u> Saturday to plan Grandmother's birthday party.

_____ **5.** My day off work is <u>the</u> day after tomorrow.

Degrees of Comparison

Adjectives and adverbs may be used to make comparisons.

ADJECTIVES: This chair is *heavy*.

              The table is *heavier*.

              That sofa is the *heaviest*.

ADVERBS: Erica edited her essay *carefully*.

              Lance edited his essay *more carefully*.

              Pauline edited her essay *most carefully*.

As you can see in the examples above, some modifiers change form to show degrees of comparison (*heavy, heavier, heaviest*). Other modifiers use *more* or *most* to show degrees of comparison (*carefully, more carefully, most carefully*).

The three degrees of comparison are **positive**, **comparative**, and **superlative**. Study the table below to see the degrees of comparison of some common modifiers.

	POSITIVE	COMPARATIVE	SUPERLATIVE
One-syllable words:	nice	nicer	nicest
	cold	colder	coldest
	high	higher	highest
Two-syllable words:	pretty	prettier	prettiest
	careful	more careful	most careful
	friendly	more friendly	most friendly
Three-syllable words:	beautiful	more beautiful	most beautiful
	difficult	more difficult	most difficult
	popular	more popular	most popular

In the table above, notice that one-syllable modifiers form the comparative degree by adding *er* and the superlative degree by adding *est*. Most one-syllable modifiers follow this pattern. Some two-syllable modifiers use *er* and *est* to form their comparative and superlative degrees. Others use *more* and *most*. Three-syllable modifiers use *more* and *most*.

ACTIVITY 4 _____

Write the comparative and superlative degrees of each modifier.

> **Samples:**
>
> | | POSITIVE | COMPARATIVE | SUPERLATIVE |
> |---|---|---|---|
> | **a.** | poor | *poorer* | *poorest* |
> | **b.** | faithful | more faithful | most faithful |

1. hot   _____   _____

2. red   _____   _____

3. tall   _____   _____

4. funny   _____   _____

5. truthful   _____   _____

6. wealthy   _____   _____

7. bravely   _____   _____

8. muscular   _____   _____

9. talented   _____   _____

10. skillfully   _____   _____

Writing Application — Using Modifiers to Make Comparisons

Using five different modifiers listed in Activity 4, write **five** sentences. You can choose any form of each modifier—positive, comparative, or superlative. Then choose **five** modifiers that are not listed in Activity 4. Use each of these modifiers in a sentence. In all of your sentences, underline the modifiers.

QUESTION: How do I make a comparison showing that one thing is less, not more, than something else?

ANSWER: Use *less* and *least* to form the comparative and superlative forms.

POSITIVE	COMPARATIVE	SUPERLATIVE
nice	less nice	least nice
pretty	less pretty	least pretty
beautiful	less beautiful	least beautiful

ACTIVITY 5

Write the comparative and superlative degrees that indicate less, not more, of each modifier.

Sample:

POSITIVE	COMPARATIVE	SUPERLATIVE
sweet	less sweet	least sweet

1. fancy _____ _____

2. expensive _____ _____

3. straight _____ _____

4. cheerful _____ _____

5. reliable _____ _____

QUESTION: What about modifiers that do not follow the regular rules to form degrees of comparison?

ANSWER: Some modifiers are irregular. Study the following table to learn their forms.

POSITIVE	COMPARATIVE	SUPERLATIVE
bad	worse	worst
badly	worse	worst
ill	worse	worst
good	better	best
well	better	best
little	less	least
many	more	most
much	more	most
far	farther *or* further	farthest *or* furthest

QUESTION: How do I know when to use each form of a modifier?

ANSWER: Follow these guidelines:

1. Use the positive degree to modify one thing. *The brown cow is* <u>*hungry*</u>.

2. Use the comparative degree to compare two things. *The brown cow is* <u>*hungrier*</u> *than the black cow.*

3. Use the superlative degree to compare three or more things. *Of the five cows, the brown cow is the* <u>*hungriest*</u>.

ACTIVITY 6

Write sentences that follow the directions below.

> **Samples:**
>
> **a.** Use the superlative degree of *generous.*
>
> Sarah is the most generous person I know.
>
> **b.** Use the comparative degree of *sour.*
>
> Is a lime less sour than a lemon?

1. Use the positive degree of *loud.*

2. Use the comparative degree of *humorous.*

3. Use the superlative degree of *impressive.*

4. Use the positive degree of *thirsty.*

5. Use the comparative degree of *angry.*

_____

6. Use the superlative degree of *original.*

_____

7. Use the comparative degree of *ill.*

_____

8. Use the superlative degree of *many.*

_____

9. Use the comparative degree of *good.*

_____

10. Use the superlative degree of *bad.*

_____

Composition Hint

When you compare one member of a group with the rest of the group, use the word *other* or *else.*

Patrick is taller than <u>anyone *else*</u> in his class. (If he was taller than *anyone* in his class, he would be taller than himself.)

This ring is less expensive than <u>any *other*</u> ring in the store. (If it was less expensive than *any* ring in the store, it would be less expensive than itself.)

ACTIVITY 7

Write sentences that compare each item below to the rest of its group.

> **Sample:**
>
> your home state
>
> _____ Florida is more beautiful than any other state. _____

1. one of your friends

_____

2. one of your school classes

_____

3. a movie

_____

4. an actor

_____

5. a song

_____

Adjectives and Adverbs Confused

Using modifiers correctly means using the proper modifier—adjective or adverb—for a particular part of speech. Study these examples of modifiers used correctly.

Daniel performed _well_ at the piano recital. (NOT _good_)

Please don't play your music so _loudly_. (NOT _loud_)

Your grandparents are _really_ happy about your grades. (NOT _real_)

Hannah wants that prom dress _badly_. (NOT _bad_)

We won that game _easily_! (NOT _easy_)

ACTIVITY 8

In each sentence, underline the correct modifier in parentheses.

> **Sample:**
>
> Why did you speak (_rude_, _rudely_) to my new friend?

1. Unwisely, he drove that car (_real, really_) fast around the curve.

2. Tabatha has read (_well, good_) since she was five years old.

3. Get over here (_quick, quickly_)!

4. Everyone laughed (_hard, hardly_) at the comedian's skit.

5. Left on the counter overnight, the fish fillets had gone (_bad, badly_).

6. How did you remain so (_brave, bravely_) during the crisis?

7. Paul always behaves (_kind, kindly_) to his little brother.

8. Vivian can work any math problem (_speedy, speedily_).

9. Dad meant well, but he burned the steaks (_bad, badly_) on the grill.

10. After much publicity, the (_real, really_) culprit was arrested and tried.

Use the clues to fill in the puzzle. Do not use spaces between words.

DOWN

1. adjective form of *reluctantly*

3. adverb meaning "in an easy way"

4. superlative degree of *festive,* showing less, not more

7. adverb form of *reliable*

8. adverb meaning "in a random manner"

9. comparative degree of *well*

10. superlative degree of *muddy*

ACROSS

2. To modify a noun, use a/an _____.

5. adjective form of *nervously*

6. positive degree of *least sure*

10. positive degree of *most*

11. adverb form of *eager*

12. This kitten is cuter than any _____ kitten.

13. positive degree of *worst*

14. comparative degree of *rarely*

15. To modify a verb, use a/an _____.

Double Negatives

A **negative** is a "no" word such as *no, not, never, nobody, nothing, hardly,* or *scarcely.* The *n't* in a contraction (such as *don't*) is a negative, too.

It is fine to use a negative in a sentence. In fact, we need to use negatives to express the idea of "no" or "not." The problem arises when we use **double negatives**.

 A *double negative* occurs when *two* negatives are mistakenly used to make one negative statement.

DOUBLE NEGATIVES: I do*n't* know *nothing* about what happened.

Raina ca*n't hardly* hit the high notes.

I ca*n't* get *no* satisfaction.

QUESTION: How do I correct a double negative?

ANSWER: Remove one of the negatives from the sentence.

NEGATIVES

Two: I don't know nothing about what happened.

One: I don't know anything about what happened.

One: I know nothing about what happened.

Two: Raina can't hardly hit the high notes.

One: Raina can hardly hit the high notes.

One: Raina almost can't hit the high notes.

Two: I can't get no satisfaction.

One: I can't get satisfaction.

One: I can get no satisfaction.

ACTIVITY 10

In each sentence, underline the correct word in parentheses.

> **Sample:**
>
> Nowadays, the wolves don't (*ever, never*) come down from the hills.

1. I don't know (*no one, anyone*) who speaks Russian.

2. You (*can, can't*) hardly believe anything Craig says.

3. Why isn't there (*no, any*) cake left for me?

4. Please don't give me (*nothing, anything*) green to eat!

5. I (*haven't, have*) met nobody my own age at this neighborhood party.

Rewrite each sentence to correct the double negative.

> **Sample:**
>
> The children haven't had no dinner yet.
>
> _____ The children haven't had dinner yet. _____

1. Marcy doesn't have no idea how to get there.

   _____

2. I hadn't scarcely finished my homework when you called.

   _____

3. You can't go nowhere until these chores are done.

   _____

4. Don't never speak to me in that tone of voice!

   _____

5. We can't hardly wait until Amy's eighteenth birthday party.

   _____

Other Problems

Besides confusing adverbs and adjectives and using double negatives, writers sometimes make other errors in usage. Follow the guidelines below to use grammar correctly.

1. Don't add _s_ to the word _anyway, anywhere, everywhere, nowhere,_ or _somewhere._

Is there a water park anywhere~~s~~ around here?

Anyway~~s~~, the mistake is yours.

2. Don't say _this here_ or _that there_ to describe a noun.

This h~~e~~re table is an heirloom from my great-grandfather.

Just lay the watermelons in that th~~e~~re tub of ice.

3. To make comparisons, don't use _more_ with an _er_ word or _most_ with an _est_ word.

My room is m~~o~~re cleaner than your room.

Lyla is the m~~o~~st smartest person in the class.

In the following passage, cross out each error in usage. If needed, write a correction above the error. Two items are completed as samples. You should find 12 additional errors.

When I heard that my ~~most~~ favorite band, Aerosmith, was coming to town, I knew I had

to get tickets. ~~Unfortunate~~ *Unfortunately*, tickets cost a lot. How would I afford them?

Immediately, I e-mailed my bestest friend, Allie. I knew that this here girl would know

how to earn money for tickets. Allie e-mailed me back right away. "Don't go anywheres," she

wrote. "I'm coming over quick."

Within five minutes, Allie was at my house. She lives closer to me than any friend. She

didn't need no car to get here, either—she just rode her bike.

She burst in the door, already describing her great idea: We should clean houses for

cash. Now, don't get me wrong, but cleaning houses sounded awfuler! But Allie had a good

point. *No one* likes to clean. Why not take advantage of this here fact?

Anyways, to make a longer story shortest, we cleaned lots of houses, we earned lots of

cash, and we had a fantastically time at the concert!

LESSON 6 Using Pronouns

As you recall from Lesson 1, a *pronoun* is a word that takes the place of a noun in a sentence. In this lesson, we will review different types of pronouns and how to use them in sentences.

Personal Pronouns

Personal pronouns are so named because, except for the pronoun *it,* they all refer to persons.

 A *personal pronoun* is used as a subject, as an object, or to show owner-ship in a sentence.

Here are the personal pronouns. A *singular* pronoun refers to one; a *plural* pronoun refers to more than one.

	SINGULAR	PLURAL
Subjective:	I	we
	you	you
	he, she, it	they
Possessive:	my, mine	our, ours
	your, yours	your, yours
	his, her, hers, its	their, theirs
Objective:	me	us
	you	you
	him, her, it	them

In the table above, the labels at the left tell how the pronouns are used in sentences. The **subjective** case pronouns are used as **subjects** in sentences.

SUBJECTIVE PRONOUNS: *We* live in a large city.

It is located on a river.

ACTIVITY 1

Complete each sentence by writing a subjective case pronoun in the blank.

> **Sample:**
>
> Have _____*you*_____ learned how to use the computer catalog at the library?

1. After school, _____ reports to a job at a fast-food restaurant.

2. Gleefully _____ waved hand-painted banners at the football game.

3. Did _____ decide to go to the community theater casting call?

4. Without a doubt, _____ are my favorite person in the whole world.

5. Where did _____ get those great-looking sunglasses?

The *possessive* case pronouns show **ownership**.

POSSESSIVE PRONOUNS: *Our* city is large.

Its location is on a river.

Mine is the best city in the world.

Note that most possessive pronouns are used as modifiers. In the first two examples above, *Our* modifies *city,* and *Its* modifies *location.* The third pronoun (*Mine*), however, is not a modifier. It is used as a noun—the subject of its sentence.

ACTIVITY 2

Complete each sentence by writing a possessive case pronoun on the blank. The hint in parentheses tells you how the pronoun is used in the sentence.

Samples:

a. Stephanie wants to cut ___her___ hair short. *(modifier)*

b. The pet boa constrictor is ___theirs___. *(noun)*

1. Is _____ locker the third one from the end? *(modifier)*

2. _____ is the best idea yet. *(noun)*

3. Somehow the dog got _____ collar off. *(modifier)*

4. Did Mr. Fuentes like _____ oral presentation? *(modifier)*

5. Is this desk _____? *(noun)*

The *objective* case pronouns are used as **objects** in sentences—specifically, as objects of prepositions, direct objects, and indirect objects.

OBJECTIVE PRONOUNS: City life is good for *us.* (object of preposition)

We love *it.* (direct object)

City life offers *me* excitement. (indirect object)

ACTIVITY 3

Complete each sentence by writing an objective case pronoun on the blank.

Sample:

Fortunately, the park ranger had drawn ___us___ a map.

1. Ms. Patterson offered _____ a study session to prepare for the SATs.

2. Otis made a mistake and graciously apologized for _____.

3. Don't tell _____ the date has been canceled!

4. Does Kinsey have a crush on _____?

5. These apples are dusty, so please wash _____.

Errors occur when writers use a pronoun in the wrong case to do a job in a sentence. For example, a pronoun used as the subject of a sentence should be in the subjective case.

> *They* <u>are</u> strict rules. (NOT *Them*)

> Fred and *I* <u>protested</u> the rules. (NOT *Fred and me*)

When you are trying to decide which pronouns to use in a compound subject, test each pronoun separately in the sentence. By doing this, you are more likely to "hear," or recognize, an incorrect usage. Then join the pronouns (or a noun and a pronoun) to form the compound subject.

> *We* <u>wrote</u> new rules. (NOT *Us*)

> *They* <u>wrote</u> new rules. (NOT *Them*)

> *We* and <u>they</u> <u>wrote</u> new rules. (NOT *Us and them*)

ACTIVITY 4

In each sentence, underline the correct pronoun in parentheses.

> **Sample:**
>
> The Hendersons and (*us,* <u>*we*</u>) have lived on this street for ten years.

1. What are (*them, they*)?

2. Reginald and (*he, him*) put new tires on the tractor.

3. After the puppet show, Joshua and (*her, she*) took a bow.

4. Did you or (*I, me*) lock the gate?

5. (*They, Them*) and their kids will come over for dinner.

A pronoun used as an object in a sentence should be in the objective case. When you are trying to decide which pronoun(s) to use in a compound object, test each pronoun separately in the sentence. Then combine them to form the compound object.

> I told <u>Harold</u> and *her* a secret. (NOT *Harold and she*)

> The secret is about *him.* (NOT *he*)

> The secret is about *me.* (NOT *I*)

> The secret is about *him* and *me.* (NOT *he and I*)

In each sentence, underline the correct pronoun in parentheses.

> **Sample:**
>
> Without Hector and (*they*, *them*), this party would have been boring.

1. The baseball sailed right over Ricardo and (*he*, *him*).

2. Give Nancy or (*me*, *I*) your money for the ticket.

3. For the yearbook, I need to photograph you and (*them*, *they*).

4. The teacher offered you and (*I*, *me*) an extra credit assignment.

5. In a moment Mom will arrive with a pizza for (*she*, *her*) and (*us*, *we*).

Agreement of Pronoun and Antecedent

A pronoun should agree with its antecedent in two ways: in *number* (singular or plural) and in *gender* (male, female, or neuter).

My *son* built *his* own bookcases. (singular, male)

Sasha focused *her* report on one star: Venus. (singular, female)

The *dog* is chasing *its* tail. (singular, neuter)

My *son* and *daughter* built *their* own bookcases.

(The antecedent *son and daughter* is plural, and the pronoun *their* is plural. Plural pronouns do not indicate gender.)

Underline the antecedent in each sentence. Then complete the sentence by writing an appropriate pronoun on the blank.

> **Samples:**
>
> a. <u>Courtney</u> invited __*her*__ two best friends over for the afternoon.
>
> b. Do all peacocks' <u>tails</u> have blue feathers in __*them*__ ?

1. Suddenly, the boat scraped _____ hull on a submerged rock.

2. Does Mrs. Otis have the grade book with _____ ?

3. Joshua and Nicole love _____ jobs at the car dealership.

4. Christopher always carries a spare ten-dollar bill with _____ .

5. All winter long, evergreens keep _____ green color.

Composition Hint

Using a masculine pronoun to refer to an antecedent that could mean a man or a woman is a practice based on outdated rules. Nowadays, many people consider this to be *sexist language,* but you can avoid this problem.

INSTEAD OF: Each *student* should write *his* name on the test booklet.

WRITE: Each *student* should write *his or her* name on the test booklet.

Do not try to correct the problem by using *their* to refer to a singular antecedent. This usage is poor grammar.

INSTEAD OF: Each *student* should write *their* name on the test booklet.

WRITE: *Students* should write *their* names on the test booklets.

ACTIVITY 7

Edit each sentence to correct sexist language or poor grammar. Make corrections by crossing out words and writing new words above them.

Samples:

a. By Friday, each employee must sign ~~his~~ *his or her* time card.

b. ~~Anyone~~ *People* paying their rent late will be charged an extra $10.

1. By Friday, every teacher should turn in his grades for the semester.

2. A child should not fear for their safety in school.

3. Each astronaut posed for his photograph in front of the space center.

4. Any mayor should have the best interests of his city at heart.

5. At the competition, every gymnast on the team tried their best.

Intensive and Reflexive Pronouns

Some pronouns combine with *self* or *selves* to form *intensive* and *reflexive pronouns.*

SINGULAR	PLURAL
myself	ourselves
himself	themselves
herself	yourselves
itself	
yourself	

An *intensive pronoun* follows a noun or pronoun and emphasizes it.

I *myself* love ice cream.

For the party, Sarah *herself* prepared the food.

James and Nora painted the house *themselves*.

A *reflexive pronoun* emphasizes its antecedent and adds information to the sentence.

I bought *myself* an ice cream cone.

(For whom did I buy a cone? For *myself*.)

Sarah threw *herself* a party.

(For whom did Sarah throw a party? For *herself*.)

James and Nora bought *themselves* a house.

(For whom did James and Nora buy a house? For *themselves*.)

ACTIVITY 8

Underline the intensive or reflexive pronoun in each sentence. Then draw an arrow to the noun or pronoun that the pronoun emphasizes.

> **Sample:**
>
> The athletes <u>themselves</u> didn't mind the rain.

1. In the fire, the roof itself was undamaged.

2. We should congratulate ourselves for a job well done.

3. Right away, the judge introduced himself to the prospective jurors.

4. Citizens organized themselves in a peaceful protest.

5. You yourself should apply for the job.

There are a few common errors involving intensive and reflexive pronouns. To avoid these errors, follow these guidelines:

1. **The words *hisself, theirself,* and *theirselves* are nonstandard. Use *himself* or *themselves* instead.**

Gregory made *himself* a sandwich. (NOT *hisself*)

The friends built *themselves* a clubhouse. (NOT *theirself*)

My parents treated *themselves* to a weekend getaway. (NOT *theirselves*)

2. Do not use *myself* in place of *I* in a compound subject.

Vince and *I* tutor middle-school students. (NOT *Vince and myself*)

3. Do not use *myself* as an object in a sentence *unless* the subject is *I*.

<u>Mr. Jenkins</u> gave Rickie and *me* a raise in pay. (NOT *Rickie and myself*)

<u>I</u> gave *myself* a pat on the back. (*Myself* is correct.)

ACTIVITY 9

Correct the pronoun errors in the following sentences. Cross out each incorrect pronoun and write the correct pronoun above it.

> **Sample:**
>   me
>   Please let Mrs. Russo and ~~myself~~ know the results.

1. The candidate hurt hisself by making that racist comment.

2. Please save seats for Betsy and myself.

3. Naturally, the winners are proud of theirselves.

4. After school, Tariq and myself ran five miles.

5. How did the boys injure theirself?

Indefinite Pronouns

Indefinite pronouns do not refer to a definite, or specific, antecedent.

 An *indefinite pronoun* takes the place of an unspecified noun.

anybody	either	neither	one
anyone	everybody	nobody	somebody
each	everyone	no one	someone

Here are examples of indefinite pronouns in sentences.

When the party got loud, *somebody* called the police.

(Somebody—we don't know who—called the police.)

Anyone may join the drama club.

(Anyone at all may join, as opposed to only specific people.)

ACTIVITY 10

On the following lines write five sentences. In each one, use an indefinite pronoun, and underline it.

> **Sample:**
>
> _____*Either would look good on you.*_____

1. _____

2. _____

3. _____

4. _____

5. _____

All indefinite pronouns are singular. Therefore, a personal pronoun that has an indefinite pronoun as an antecedent must be singular.

Everybody cast *his* or *her* vote. (NOT *their votes*)

Each has a label on *its* lid. (NOT *their lids*)

ACTIVITY 11

Underline the indefinite pronoun in each sentence. Then underline the personal pronoun, or pronoun pair, that agrees with it.

> **Samples:**
>
> **a.** <u>One</u> had pinstripes along (*its*, *their*) side.
>
> **b.** Did <u>anyone</u> want (*their*, *his or her*) photograph taken?

1. Does anybody have a red marker with (*them, him or her*)?

2. Each had a yellow ribbon tied around (*them, it*).

3. In my opinion, neither expressed (*his or her, their*) true feelings.

4. Everyone should pack (*their, his or her*) suitcase as lightly as possible.

5. Nobody thought to bring spare clothing for (*himself or herself, themselves*).

Composition Hint

On its own, an indefinite pronoun does not indicate gender.

Someone left *his or her* tennis racket on the bench. (NOT *his*)

Often, however, you can compose sentences that indicate the gender of indefinite pronouns. As a result, your sentence is more clear and specific.

Someone on the girls' tennis team left *her* racket on the bench.

Rewrite each sentence, making the gender of the indefinite pronoun clear. Use an appropriate personal pronoun to refer to the indefinite pronoun.

Sample:

Someone said he or she enjoyed reading *Pride and Prejudice.*

Someone in the women's book club said she enjoyed reading Pride and Prejudice.

1. Everybody at the school wore his or her new uniform.

_____

2. No one offered to lend me his or her baseball glove.

_____

3. Each paid for his or her own lunch.

_____

4. Someone demonstrated his or her impressive jump shot.

_____

5. One accidentally got paint on his or her hands.

_____

Since indefinite pronouns are singular, they always take singular verbs.

Neither <u>is</u> my first choice.

<u>Was</u> <u>anyone</u> home?

Remember, a phrase that comes between the subject and verb does not affect the agreement of the subject and verb.

<u>Neither</u> of the applicants <u>is</u> my first choice.

(The verb *is* agrees with the subject *Neither,* not with the prepositional object *applicants.*)

Underline the correct form of the verb in parentheses.

Sample:

Everyone in the first five rows (<u>*has,*</u> *have*) season tickets.

1. Each of the dogs (*need, needs*) a warm, soapy bath.

2. Anyone with large deliveries (*enters, enter*) through the back door.

3. (*Do, Does*) either of these books seem interesting?

4. Fortunately, no one really (*believe, believes*) the rumor about me.

5. (*Is, Are*) one of these poems your favorite?

ACTIVITY 14

The French philosopher and author Jean-Paul Sartre was awarded the Nobel Prize in literature in 1964—but he refused to accept the prize. To find out how he explained his refusal, unscramble the sentence below.

Drop the letters from each vertical column—not necessarily in the order in which they appear—into the empty boxes below them to spell words. The quotation reads from left to right, line by line. Black squares indicate ends of words.

After you unscramble the quotation, write it on the lines provided.

A	B	E	R	T	R	T	R	W	U	O	I	M	N	E	E	I	N	T	O
A	T	W	I	A	T	A	O	T	M	H	I	O	S	D	L	F	U	S	O
	N	O		N	L	E	I		F	U	R	T				F			

			I					S		R			E
				L					M				
				N	S				E			T	
			S			T							

_____

_____

— *Jean-Paul Sartre*

ACTIVITY 15

Now that you have unscrambled Sartre's words, answer the following questions.

1. Which word in the sentence is a pronoun? _____

2. What kind of pronoun is this word? _____

3. Explain why Sartre's choice of words could be considered sexist language.

_____

_____

4. Revise the sentence to correct the sexist language.

_____

_____

5. What do you think Sartre's statement means, exactly? Look up unfamiliar words in a dictionary to understand Sartre's full meaning. Then write your interpretation of his statement below.

_____

_____

_____

In this book, Lesson 14 discusses a small group of pronouns called relative pronouns, which are used to introduce a certain type of subordinate clause.

Review of Using Verbs, Modifiers, and Pronouns

To use **verbs** correctly in sentences, remember these key points:

(a) Use the *verb tense* that accurately expresses the *time* of the action (when it occurred).

(b) Use *consistent verb tense* within a piece of writing, whether it is a sentence, paragraph, or longer piece. Switch to a different tense only if the time of the action changes.

(c) Make the verb *agree* with its subject in number (singular verb or plural verb).

ACTIVITY 1 _____

Complete the table below by filling in the missing parts of each verb. A sample is completed for you.

	BASE FORM	PRESENT PARTICIPLE	PAST	PAST PARTICIPLE
	choose	(is) _choosing_	_chose_	(has) _chosen_
1.	accept	(is) _____	_____	(has) _____
2.	affect	(is) _____	_____	(has) _____
3.	become	(is) _____	_____	(has) _____
4.	lay	(is) _____	_____	(has) _____
5.	set	(is) _____	_____	(has) _____
6.	speak	(is) _____	_____	(has) _____
7.	swim	(is) _____	_____	(has) _____
8.	take	(is) _____	_____	(has) _____
9.	teach	(is) _____	_____	(has) _____
10.	write	(is) _____	_____	(has) _____

On the lines below, write ten sentences using past and past participle verb forms from Activity 1. Underline each verb in your sentences.

1. _____

2. _____

3. _____

4. _____

5. _____

6. _____

7. _____

8. _____

9. _____

10. _____

To use **modifiers** correctly in sentences, remember these key points:

(a) An *adjective* modifies a noun or a pronoun.

(b) An *adverb* modifies a verb, adjective, or adverb.

(c) Use the *positive* degree of comparison to modify one thing (*tall* girl), the *comparative* degree to compare two things (She is *taller* than I), and the *superlative* degree to compare more than two things (the *tallest* student in the class).

(d) Avoid these errors: double negatives; adding *s* to *anywhere, somewhere,* etc.; using *this here* or *that there* to modify a noun; using *more* with a comparative ending in *er* (*taller,* not *more taller*); using *most* with a superlative ending in *est* (*tallest,* not *most tallest*).

To use **pronouns** correctly in sentences, remember these key points:

(a) The *personal pronouns,* except for *it,* refer to persons. Personal pronouns are used as subjects or objects in sentences, or to show possession.

(b) Make a pronoun agree with its antecedent in *number* and *gender.*

(c) An *intensive* or *reflexive pronoun* adds emphasis to the noun or pronoun it follows.

(d) Don't use nonstandard words like *hisself, theirself,* and *theirselves.*

In the following passage, numbered blanks show where words have been left out of sentences. Look at the item that corresponds with each blank and circle the letter of the best word or words to complete the sentence.

from "Paul's Case"
Willa Cather

It was Paul's afternoon to appear before the faculty of the Pittsburgh High School to account for his various misdemeanors. He __(1)__ a week ago, and his __(2)__ had called at the Principal's office and confessed his perplexity about his son. Paul entered the faculty room suave and smiling. . . .

When questioned by the Principal as to why he was there, Paul stated, __(3)__ enough, that he wanted to come back to school. This __(4)__ a lie, but Paul was quite accustomed to lying; found it, indeed, indispensable for overcoming friction. His teachers __(5)__ to state their respective charges against him, which they did with such a rancor and aggrievedness as evinced that this was not a usual case. Disorder and impertinence __(6)__ among the offenses named, yet each of his instructors felt that it __(7)__ possible to put into words the real cause of the trouble, which __(8)__ in a sort of hysterically defiant manner of the boy's; in the contempt which they all knew he felt for __(9)__, and which he seemingly made not the __(10)__ to conceal.

1. A. is suspended
   B. will be suspended
   C. had been suspended

2. D. father
   E. mother
   F. stepmother

3. A. politely
   B. polite
   C. most polite

4. D. is
   E. was
   F. will be

5. A. is asked
   B. were asked
   C. has been asked

6. D. was
   E. is
   F. were

7. A. was not scarcely
   B. wasn't scarcely
   C. was scarcely

8. D. lay
   E. lies
   F. laid

9. A. them
   B. they
   C. him or her

10. D. less effort
    E. least effort
    F. leastest effort

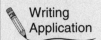

Writing Application

Using Verbs, Modifiers, and Pronouns

In the excerpt from "Paul's Case," in Activity 3, Paul believes that telling lies is "indispensable for overcoming friction." First of all, what do you think Paul means, exactly? And second, do you agree with Paul?

Write **two** paragraphs, answering these two questions. Use examples from real life to help explain your answers. Check your work carefully for the correct use of verbs, modifiers, and pronouns.

ACTIVITY 4

Use the comparative or superlative degree of each modifier below in a sentence. (Remember, you can use *more/most* or *less/least* to form comparative and superlative degrees.)

1. *funny* _____

_____

2. *slowly* _____

_____

3. *loudly* _____

_____

4. *aggressive* _____

_____

5. *heavy* _____

_____

ACTIVITY 5

In each sentence, underline the correct word in parentheses.

1. Since elementary school, Elton and (*I, me, myself*) have loved airplanes.

2. Parents have always (*brung, brought, bringed*) snacks to the PTA meetings.

3. How did you finish your science project so (*quick, quickly, quicker*)?

4. In my opinion, Ms. Henry is nicer than (*any, any other, all*) teacher at this school.

5. Did a package come in the mail for my sister and (*I, me, myself*)?

6. (*This here, That there, This*) vine is called poison oak; it causes an itchy rash on skin.

7. I don't want to hear (*no, any, hardly no*) excuses about cleaning your room!

8. Although Bobby looked (*everywhere, everywheres*) for the book, he couldn't find it.

9. Either Molly or Nan will present (*her, their, its*) oral report first.

10. Each of these puppies (*have been, has been*) vaccinated and registered with the city.

11. Charlie, you (*is, are, was*) scheduled to work on Friday night, okay?

12. How on earth did Samuel lock (*himself, hisself, herself*) in the utility room?

13. Under bright lights (*were, are, is*) the star of the show.

14. Your daughter has chicken pox, but she will be (*better, more better, best*) soon.

15. Each of the lawyers refused to discuss (*his, their, his or her*) case with the press.

16. One of the boys in AP English got (*his, their, his or her*) short story published in a magazine.

17. My older sister and her husband have opened a savings account for (*theirselves, themselves, theirself*).

18. This summer, (*them, their, they*) and Will are coaching Little League.

19. The cupcake, plus the rich frosting, (*have, has, is having*) a lot of fatty calories.

20. Obediently Jessie swept the floor, and then he (*do, does, did*) the dishes.

Using Grammar

It's time to take a break from traditional grammar exercises. The following activities ask you to explore how people use grammar in the real world, outside your classroom walls. Which activity sparks your interest? Choose an activity to complete; then, with your teacher's approval, share the results with your classmates. Have a good time!

Now Crispier!

How do advertisers use the degrees of comparison? Do a study of what kinds of things are compared—products, qualities, consumer preferences, and so on. Then examine how advertisers phrase the comparisons. For example, why do they sometimes use open-ended comparisons, such as "Now crispier!"? (You are left to wonder, Crispier than what?) Write a summary of your findings, giving examples of comparisons in advertisements along with your own analysis of why ads are worded this way.

Oh, Don't Nobody Love Me?

Take a few days to listen—really listen—to the lyrics in songs. How many grammar errors can you collect? Make a list of grammar errors, along with the songs and artists responsible. Then think about how each error affects you as a listener. Does it interfere with your understanding? Create a particular mood? Send a message about the speaker in the song, or about the artist?

Local Color

Find out about the local color movement in American literature. When was the local color movement? What qualities define local color writing? Who are some of the authors who wrote in this style? And, most important, how do these authors use grammar in characters' speech to help show local color?

Check It Out

Many people rely on grammar-check software to find the grammar errors in their writing. How reliable is this method of finding errors? Is the software "blind" to certain kinds of errors? Does it always suggest the best correction? Perform a test of grammar-check software to see how it responds to the kinds of errors discussed in Lessons 3–6. Based on your findings, what recommendations do you have for writers?

Prima Donna

The dumb jock, the ditzy cheerleader, the country bumpkin, the rich snob—these are just a few stereotypes. Does one of these stereotypes, or some other one, strike you as particularly unfair? Prepare a defense of this kind of person—an athlete, for example, or a politician. Present a summary of the stereotype, then show how real-life individuals of this sort are not stereotypical. Pay special attention to how the use of grammar affects a stereotype. (Do all professional football players use double negatives, for example?)

Careers

Job descriptions rarely specify that applicants be able to use grammar correctly. Does this mean that grammar is unimportant in most jobs? Examine five different careers that interest you and decide how important correct grammar is in each job. Give examples of responsibilities and activities that support your analysis.

Slow Children at Play

The careless—or uninformed—use of modifiers, verbs, and pronouns sometimes leads to unexpected humor. Read signs in your town or city or surf the Internet to find humorous errors or interpretations. Write a short skit or dialogue, using the sign/sentence as a punch line, or create a cartoon drawing or comic strip inspired by the humorous error. How would you rewrite the sign or sentence to make its meaning more clear and specific?

8 Using Punctuation

Writing sentences correctly means using correct grammar, but it also means using correct punctuation. Truthfully, an entire workbook could be devoted just to punctuation rules. However, mastery of a few basic rules will help you avoid the most common errors.

PUNCTUATION MARK	WHAT IT DOES	EXAMPLE
comma (,)	With a conjunction, it joins sentences.	I adjusted the camera lens, *and* I took an amazing photograph.
	It separates items in a series.	Jamar researched careers in *education, law,* and *medicine.*
		Zelda scattered birdseed *beneath the tree, near the birdbath,* and *in the grass.*
	It sets off an introductory word, phrase, or clause.	*Fortunately,* I made a backup copy of my report on T. S. Eliot.
		In the introductory paragraph, I introduce my topic and state my thesis.
		After I wrote the report, I revised it to correct grammar mistakes.
	It sets off interrupting words and expressions.	The umpire's decision, *in my opinion,* was fair.
		To be honest, I do not need your help.
semicolon (;)	It joins sentences.	I wrote the essay today; tomorrow, I'll edit it. (no conjunction)
		Hilary writes poetry; *however,* the poems aren't very good. (conjunctive adverb)
	It joins items in a series when one or more items have a comma.	His destinations include *Carson City, Nevada; Lincoln, Nebraska;* and *San Diego.*
colon (:)	It calls attention to what follows.	The nominees are these: Halle Berry, Lucy Liu, and Nicole Kidman.
apostrophe (')	With *s,* it forms the possessive of singular words and of plurals not ending in *s.*	car**'s** engine, someone**'s** books men**'s** locker room, geese**'s** feathers
	It forms the possessive of plural words ending in *s.*	several cars' engines a few friends' messages
	It forms contractions.	haven't, I've, they'll, we're

quotation marks("...")	A pair of them encloses direct quotations.	Morgan said, "I have tickets to the new Will Smith movie." "Great!" I responded.
	A pair of them encloses the titles of short works.	"A Rose for Emily," "The Star-Spangled Banner," "Life in the Big Leagues"
italics (or <u>underlining</u>)	They punctuate the titles of longer works.	*The Scarlet Letter*, <u>Sports Illustrated</u>, *Schindler's List*, <u>Pittsburgh Post-Gazette</u>

ACTIVITY 1

Insert commas, semicolons, and colons where they are needed.

> **Samples:**
>
> **a.** *The Last Samurai,* starring Tom Cruise, was nominated for three Academy Awards.
>
> **b.** My passion is sports; therefore, I am looking forward to watching the Olympic Games.
>
> **c.** Drew Barrymore has found success in the following areas: acting, producing, and writing.

1. Joe DiMaggio was the son of Italian immigrants he rose to fame playing baseball in the 1930s and '40s.

2. Reese Witherspoon has starred in *Cruel Intentions Sweet Home Alabama* and *Legally Blonde.*

3. Please write a short biography of one of these hockey players Wayne Gretzky Bobby Hull or James Craig.

4. Enrique Iglesias like his father sings in both English and Spanish.

5. A few fabulous authors are these Toni Morrison Gary Paulsen Amy Tan and Paul Zindel.

6. I wasn't sure I would enjoy a concert by Coldplay nevertheless, I agreed to go with my friends.

7. This issue of *Teen People* features articles on Shane West an actor Christina Aguilera a singer and Michael Phelps an Olympic swimmer.

8. The Women's National Basketball Association (WNBA) was formed in 1997 it has been going strong ever since.

9. OutKast not Missy Elliott won the Grammy for Album of the Year in 2004.

10. Venus Williams and Serena Williams are stylish sisters but they are also amazing, famous tennis players.

Composition Hint

When you begin a sentence with a prepositional phrase, the rule of thumb is to put a comma after the phrase (see the table of punctuation rules on pages 77–78). However, you can use your judgment to leave out the comma if the prepositional phrase is only a few words long (say, two to four words).

NO COMMA: *In the poem* Prufrock asks, "Do I dare/Disturb the universe?"

(This short prepositional phrase stands out clearly as a single unit of thought. Because it is short and simple, readers easily take in its meaning and notice where the phrase ends and the subject of the sentence begins.)

COMMA: *In the poem's sixth stanza,* Prufrock asks, "Do I dare/Disturb the universe?"

(This phrase is longer and more complicated, causing readers to slow down and think. The comma is a helpful reading aid marking a clear separation of the introductory phrase and *Prufrock,* the subject of the sentence. The comma also helps emphasize the information in the phrase by causing readers to pause briefly after reading it.)

When you begin a sentence with two (or more) prepositional phrases in a row, put a comma after the final phrase.

COMMA: *In line 122* *of the poem,* Prufrock asks, "Do I dare to eat a peach?"

When a prepositional phrase begins a sentence in which the verb comes before the subject, do not use a comma.

NO COMMA: *In line 122* is the question about the peach.

(The verb *is* comes before the subject *question.* Do not set off the introductory prepositional phrase with a comma.)

Writing
Application

Using Commas With Prepositional Phrases

Imagine that you are writing an e-mail to a friend, telling him or her how you would set up the ideal family room. Write **five** sentences that begin with prepositional phrases of various lengths to describe how you would set up the room, but for now, do *not* use commas after the introductory phrases. For example, you might write, *Underneath the room's big window I would set up a table for playing board games.*

With your teacher's approval, exchange papers with a classmate. Read your classmate's sentences and decide which ones need a comma after the introductory phrase(s). Insert the needed commas, then discuss the results with your classmate.

Composition Hint

You can use a special kind of interrupter called an *appositive* to add crucial information to your sentences easily. An appositive is a word or word group that renames or identifies the noun or pronoun it follows.

Mordicai Gerstein, *a talented artist*, won the Caldecott Medal in 2004.

I'd like to introduce the winner, *Mordicai Gerstein*.

Notice that an appositive is set off by a pair of commas or a single comma, depending on its place in the sentence.

Writing Application

Using Appositives

You are a talk-show host, and you are writing a script to introduce **five** guests on tonight's show. Write five or more sentences to introduce your dream guests, and use an appositive to include vital information about each person.

ACTIVITY 2

On the line provided, write the possessive form of each word.

Samples:

a. grass   *grass's*

b. workers   *workers'*

1. heart _____   6. Louisiana _____

2. people _____   7. piano _____

3. sisters _____   8. pianos _____

4. bus _____   9. mice _____

5. buses _____   10. college _____

QUESTION: When I use quotation marks in sentences, do I place other punctuation marks inside or outside the quotation marks?

ANSWER: It depends. Follow these guidelines:

(a) A period or a comma goes inside a closing quotation mark.

Wilson Mizner said, "Hollywood is a trip through a sewer in a glass-bottomed boat."

"Success and failure are equally disastrous," said Tennessee Williams.

(b) An exclamation point or question mark goes inside the closing quotation mark if it is part of the direct quotation. Otherwise, it goes outside.

Regarding life as a writer, Ring Lardner said, "How can you write if you can't cry?"

(The quoted words ask a question, so the question mark is inside the quotation mark.)

Why did H. L. Mencken say, "There are no dull subjects. There are only dull writers"?

(The entire sentence, not the quoted words, asks a question, so the question mark is outside the quotation mark.)

QUESTION: What about using quotation marks in dialogue within a story?

ANSWER: In dialogue, punctuate each speaker's words separately. Otherwise, follow the rules above.

Aida asked, "Who was Ring Lardner Jr.?"

"He was a novelist and screenwriter," Ms. Thompson answered. "He wrote, among other things, the Academy Award–winning screenplay *M*A*S*H*."

ACTIVITY 3

Add quotation marks exactly where they are needed in the following passage. One pair of quotation marks is already inserted as a sample.

Jared pops his skateboard up and catches it. "I hate the new city law," he says.

You mean the one about no skateboarding allowed in public parking lots? says

Nick.

That's the one, says Jared, grimacing. Now we'll have to break the law just to

use a skateboard. Pretty soon, the newspapers will run stories about juvenile delin-

quents and their boards. This isn't fair!

I have an idea, says Nick. I was surfing the Net the other day, and I found

some sites about skateboard parks. In other cities, people have remodeled old

roller-skating rinks into indoor skateboard parks. Some cities have even built awe-

some outdoor parks.

You think we could get something like that in our city? says Nick.

If there's enough interest, some businessperson would love to make money off

a skate park, says Jared. If not, we'll take business courses in college and do it

ourselves!

Answer each question by writing a title on the line provided. Punctuate each title using quotation marks or underlining.

What Do Your Tastes in Entertainment Say About You?

Take this easy quiz to find out!

What is . . .

1. the last book you read by choice? _____

2. your favorite movie? _____

3. the album in your CD player right now? _____

4. a short story you would read more than once? _____

5. a movie you'd go to on a date? _____

6. your favorite magazine? _____

7. the last song that got stuck in your head? _____

8. a newspaper/magazine article you read all the way through? _____

9. a play that reminds you of your own life? _____

10. a poem you'd love to know by heart? _____

What do your answers mean? If you named mainly . . .

action-oriented titles, you are the sort to grab life by the horns and find your own fun. Others gravitate to you, drawn by your energy and excitement. Enjoy the attention, but do not be afraid to seek out a quiet pal who exudes calm.

romantic titles, you are the sort who looks for the good in life and in others. Your generosity, compassion, and bright outlook help others be their best. Do not be afraid to admit that your best asset is your heart!

humorous titles, you are the sort who sees the glass as half full, and if it is not, you will add water to make it that way. You have never met a stranger, but few people know your true dreams and emotions. Do not be afraid to open up to someone special.

Using Contractions

In informal writing, contractions help to set a conversational tone. You see contractions used in dialogue in novels, short stories, plays, and many magazine articles.

Edit the text in Activity 4 under the heading "What do your answers mean?" Cross out words that could be joined in a contraction and write the contraction above the words. Be sure to use apostrophes to form contractions correctly.

Using Capitalization

Like punctuation rules, capitalization rules are numerous. Study the guidelines in the following table to help yourself avoid the most common mistakes.

CAPITALIZE . . .	EXAMPLES
the first word in a sentence.	**H**ave you read anything by Victor Hugo?
the pronoun *I*.	Last summer, **I** read one of his plays.
the first word in a direct quotation.	Ms. Bellsy told us, "**T**he author of *Les Misérables* is Victor Hugo."
proper nouns, their abbreviations, and proper adjectives.	**V**ictor **H**ugo, **F**rance, **E**urope, **P**aris, **L**eaning **T**ower of **P**isa, **R**hine **R**iver, **S**eptember, **S**ept., **M**r., **P**rof., **A**ve., **C**orp., **I**nc. **F**rench, **E**uropean, **P**arisian
the first and all main words in titles.	*The **H**unchback of **N**otre **D**ame* (book) "**B**e **L**ike the **B**ird" (poem) *The **K**ing **T**akes **H**is **A**musement* (play) "**W**hat **Y**ou **D**idn't **K**now **A**bout **H**ugo" (article)
the first word and all nouns in the salutation, and the first word in the closing of a letter.	**D**ear **M**r. **H**ugo: **D**ear **G**randfather, **S**incerely yours, **Y**our grandson,

ACTIVITY 1

Answer each question, writing your answer on the line provided.

> **Sample:**
>
> Name one of the planets in our solar system. _____Saturn_____

1. Name a river in the United States. _____

2. What city—anywhere in the world—would you like to visit? _____

3. What is one of America's national parks? _____

4. Name your favorite U.S. president. _____

5. Who is your English class teacher? _____

6. What is the street, city, and state of your residence? _____

7. Write the abbreviation of your favorite month. _____

8. What proper adjective is formed from *Persia*? _____

9. Write the salutation of a letter to a family member. _____

10. Write the closing of a letter from yourself. _____

11. What day of the week is today? _____

12. How is the noun in item 11 abbreviated? _____

13. In a business name, how would *Company* be abbreviated? _____

14. Name a poem that you have read recently. _____

15. What is a good title for an article about airline safety?

_____

ACTIVITY 2 _____

In the following story excerpt and its title, cross out each lowercase letter that should be capitalized and write the capital letter above it. As a sample, the author's name has been corrected for you.

Earlier in this story, Mathilde borrowed a necklace from Madame Forestier and then lost it. Now, the women meet unexpectedly, after not having seen each other for years.

from "the necklace"

G̶uy de m̶aupassant

her friend uttered a cry.

"oh, my poor mathilde! how you are changed!"

"yes, i have had days hard enough, since i have seen you, days wretched enough—and that because of you!"

"of me! how so?"

"do you remember that diamond necklace which you lent me to wear at the ministerial ball?"

"yes. well?"

"well, i lost it."

"what do you mean? you brought it back."

"i brought you back another just like it. and for this we have been ten years paying. you can understand that it was not easy for us, us who had nothing. at last it is ended, and i am very glad."

mme. forestier had stopped.

"you say that you bought a necklace of diamonds to replace mine?"

"yes. you never noticed it, then! they were very like."

and she smiled with a joy which was proud and naïve at once.

mme. forestier, strongly moved, took her two hands.

"oh, my poor mathilde! why, my necklace was paste. it was worth at most five hundred francs!"

Writing Application Using Capitalization to Write About Poetry

Read the following poem, then follow the instructions below it.

Be Like the Bird
Victor Hugo

Be like the bird who

Halting in his flight

On limb too slight

Feels it give way beneath him,

Yet sings

Knowing he hath wings.

What is your interpretation of the poem's advice to "Be like the bird"? How does this advice apply to your life?

On a separate sheet of paper, write **two** paragraphs answering these questions. Use quotations from the poem and examples from your life to explain your interpretation. Then check your work for the correct use of capitalization and punctuation.

When it comes to capitalization, some kinds of nouns can be challenging. The following guidelines will help you capitalize these words correctly.

1. The words *sun* and *moon* are not capitalized except as the first word in a sentence. The word *earth* is capitalized only when discussed as a specific planet.

> Dorothy's house fell to earth with a thump.

> Besides **E**arth, humans have set foot on the moon but not **M**ars.

2. The names of the seasons are not capitalized.

> Which is your favorite season—spring, summer, autumn, or winter?

3. Capitalize the names of specific sections of the country.

> the **S**outheast, the **N**orthwest, the **S**outhwest

> The **N**ortheast is densely populated.

Do not capitalize these names if they are merely compass points.

> The subway station is on the northeast corner of Main and Fifth.

4. Capitalize words used as a name or used before a name in direct address.

> **D**ad, **M**other, **U**ncle **S**hen, **G**randma, **C**ousin **A**bisha

> Good morning, **M**om.

Do not capitalize *mom, dad,* or titles such as *aunt* following a possessive pronoun.

> My dad will drive me to work, and my uncle will pick me up later.

5. Capitalize the names of language courses and numbered courses.

       English, **S**panish, **F**rench, **R**ussian

       Algebra 2, **M**athematics 4, **P**hotography 101

Do not capitalize the names of unnumbered courses, except for languages.

       history, advanced chemistry, world cultures, biology

ACTIVITY 3

Cross out each lowercase letter that should be a capital and write the capital letter above it. If a sentence needs no correction, write *C* for *correct* on the blank.

Samples:

_____ **a.** When I spoke to u̶ncle r̶amiro, he said he was picking up Chinese food.

___*C*__ **b.** Tell your dad that you're staying overnight at my house.

_____ **1.** Was your vacation to the northwest enjoyable?

_____ **2.** Jonathan plans to become a high-school football coach like our dad.

_____ **3.** In the summer, Bastien usually works at the YMCA as a camp counselor.

_____ **4.** Where on earth have you been?

_____ **5.** Ginger plans to invite cousin Aimee to our house for dinner.

_____ **6.** Where did you go to college, aunt Nasrin?

_____ **7.** Which two planets lie between earth and the sun?

_____ **8.** José was finally tackled in the southeast corner of the field.

_____ **9.** Did you get the message I left with your mom?

_____ **10.** As a senior, Meghan will take history IV.

ACTIVITY 4

Write the names of five courses you are taking in school this semester.

1. _____

2. _____

3. _____

4. _____

5. _____

Using Capitalization in Travel Writing

Each week, the *New York Times* runs a feature called "36 Hours in _____." The blank is filled in with the name of a different city, and the article describes in detail what a visitor can do, eat, see, and experience during a 36-hour stay in this city.

Use the *Times* feature as inspiration and write your own travel article. The city is up to you. Focusing on your own hometown may be easiest, but choosing a distant city may be more inspiring. Either way, include lots of proper nouns and at least one proper adjective. Give your article a title and, of course, check your work for the correct use of capitalization.

ACTIVITY 5

Decide whether each word in the box is a proper noun, common noun, proper adjective, or common adjective. Write the word, using correct punctuation, in the appropriate column. Then fit the words into the puzzle. Four letters are already inserted in the puzzle to help you get started.

western african banner day hindu jeffersonian street greek federal islander

egyptian taiwan sunny latin senator sun swiss montana

DOWN

ACROSS

Proper Nouns and Proper Adjectives   *Common Nouns and Common Adjectives*

_____   _____

_____   _____

_____   _____

_____   _____

_____   _____

_____   _____

_____   _____

_____   _____

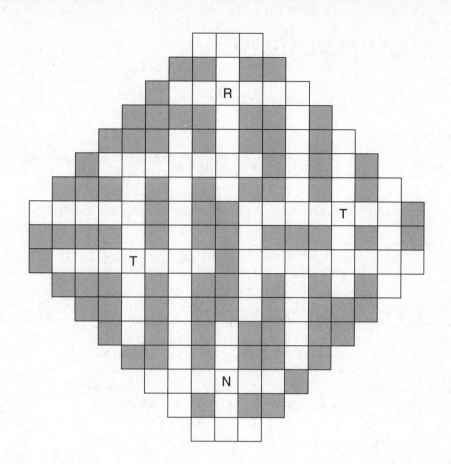

10 Using Spelling

The following simple rules can help you to spell a great many words correctly.

Helpful Spelling Rules

RULE	EXAMPLES
Write *i* before *e* except after *c*, or when sounded like *a* as in *neighbor* and *weigh*.	ni**e**ce, chi**e**f, fi**e**ld, achi**e**ve conc**ei**t, rec**ei**pt, c**ei**ling, rec**ei**ve
When adding a **prefix**, do not change the spelling of the original word.	co + operate = cooperate non + sense = nonsense semi + circle = semicircle
When adding the **suffix *ly*** or ***ness***, do not change the spelling of the original word. *Exception:* Words ending in a consonant and *y*. See rule below.	legal + ly = legal**ly** neat + ly = neat**ly** great + ness = great**ness** glad + ness = glad**ness**
When a word ends in a **consonant and *y*,** change the *y* to *i* before a suffix not beginning with *i*. When a word ends in a **vowel and *y*,** keep the *y* when adding a suffix.	hairy + ness = hair**i**ness happy + ly = happ**i**ly fly + ing = fl**y**ing terrify + ing = terrif**y**ing joy + ous = jo**y**ous
When a word ends in a **silent *e*** . . . . . . drop the *e* to add a suffix beginning with a vowel. . . . keep the *e* to add a suffix beginning with a consonant.	skate + ing = skat**ing** write + er = writ**er** amaze + ment = amaz**e**ment hope + ful = hop**e**ful
Double the final consonant before a suffix beginning with a vowel if the word is one-syllable or is accented on the final syllable. **Do not double the consonant** if it is preceded by more than one vowel.	snug + er = snu**gg**er snap + y = sna**pp**y unplug + ing = unplu**gg**ing clean + est = clean**est** sleep + er = slee**p**er

---

ACTIVITY 1 _____

Add the prefix or suffix to each word and write the new word on the line provided.

> **Samples:**
>
> **a.** pre + view = _____*preview*_____   **b.** inside + er = _____*insider*_____

1. nervous + ly = _____

2. re + group = _____

3. personal + ly = _____

4. hazy + ly = _____

5. de + form = _____

6. refuse + ing = _____

7. bag + y = _____

8. destroy + ed = _____

9. mono + rail = _____

10. barren + ness = _____

ACTIVITY 2

Underline the correct spelling of each word in parentheses.

Should teenagers under age eighteen be (*legaly, legally*) required to have a parent's consent before (*using, useing*) a tanning booth? The mere idea of such a law is sure to irk some teens. After all, aren't the teen years already (*packed, packked*) full of prohibitions?

Teens who balk at (*geting, getting*) a parent or guardian's permission to tan may be surprised to hear this: Some lawmakers (*believe, beleive*) teens should be banned from tanning booths (*entirely, entirly*). In 2004, California assemblyman Joe Nation wrote a bill to make it (*ilegal, illegal*) for young people under eighteen to use tanning salons in his state. Why? (*Exposure, Exposesure*) to the sun's ultraviolet rays can lead to skin cancer, just as (*smoking, smokeing*) cigarettes may lead to cancer. Since teens under age eighteen are prohibited from (*buyyng, buying*) tobacco products, it follows logically that they should also be prohibited from using tanning booths.

 Writing Application

Using Spelling Rules

What is your opinion on the topic of teens and tanning booths? Do you think they should be free to tan if they want to? Or do you agree that requiring permission from an adult is reasonable? Or, taking things to a greater extreme, do you think teens should be protected by law from tanning booths, just as they are protected from smoking and drinking?

Write **two** paragraphs explaining your point of view on teens, tanning, and laws. Back up your opinion with reasons and examples. Then check your writing for words that follow the spelling rules in the table above and underline each of these words.

Spelling the Plurals of Nouns

SPELLING RULE	EXAMPLES
For **most nouns**, add *s* to the singular to form the plural.	raisin**s**, shoestring**s**, motor**s**, note**s**, message**s**, computer**s**, snack**s**
For nouns ending in *s, sh, ch*, or *x*, add *es* to form the plural.	pass**es**, crash**es**, patch**es**, box**es**
For most nouns ending in *f*, change *f* to *v* and add *es* to form the plural. For a few nouns ending in *f*, add *s*.	leaf, lea**ves** thief, thie**ves** roof, roof**s** belief, belief**s**
For three nouns ending in *fe*—**knife, life, wife**—change *f* to *v* and add *s* to form the plural.	kni**fe**, kni**ves** li**fe**, li**ves** wi**fe**, wi**ves**
For nouns ending in a **consonant plus *y***, change the *y* to *i* and add *es*.	enem**y**, enem**ies** compan**y**, compan**ies**
For nouns ending in *o*, add *s* in most cases. For some nouns ending in a consonant plus *o*, add *es*.	video**s**, piano**s**, soprano**s**, memento**s**, radio**s** tomato/tomato**es**, potato/potato**es**
Some nouns form their plurals **irregularly**.	child, children ox, oxen crisis, crises parenthesis, parentheses datum, data series, series deer, deer sheep, sheep foot, feet shrimp, shrimp goose, geese syllabus, syllabi louse, lice thesis, theses man, men tooth, teeth medium, media woman, women moose, moose mouse, mice

ACTIVITY 3

Write the plural of each word on the line provided.

Samples:

a. wax _____*waxes*_____   **b.** moose _____*moose*_____

1. tax _____   6. half _____

2. lunch _____   7. mouse _____

3. cuff _____   8. life _____

4. rash _____   9. alto _____

5. salary _____   10. grief _____

ACTIVITY 4 _____

Use the blocks to build singular nouns of four or six letters. Use each block only once and write the words on the lines provided. Then use the plural form of each word in a sentence.

Singular Nouns Associated with Cities

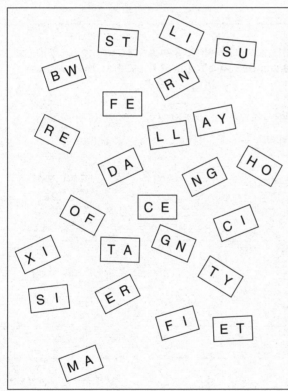

1. __ __ __ __
2. __ __ __ __
3. __ __ __ __
4. __ __ __ __
5. __ __ __ __
6. __ __ __ __
7. __ __ __ __
8. __ __ __ __
9. __ __ __ __
10. __ __ __ __ __ __

11. _____

12. _____

13. _____

14. _____

15. _____

16. _____

17. _____

18. _____

19. _____

20. _____

Composition Hint

When people write plurals, one of the most common errors they make is using an apostrophe to form a plural. Remember that an apostrophe is not used to form plurals.

    five employees (NOT employee's)

    three Mondays (NOT Monday's)

ACTIVITY 5

The following is a list of nouns. On the lines provided, write sentences using the plural form of five of the nouns. Then use the possessive form of the other five nouns to write five more sentences.

~~essay~~	~~shoe~~	promise	keyboard	comedy	accomplishment
week	dancer	Friday	visitor	shopper	participant

Samples:

a. My history teacher assigned two essays in one semester.

b. For prom, I matched the shoe's color to the dress.

Plural Nouns

1. _____

2. _____

3. _____

4. _____

5. _____

Possessive Nouns

6. _____

7. _____

8. _____

9. _____

10. _____

Frequently Misspelled Words

The commonly used words in the following list are among the most frequently misspelled.
Review them and master them!

ache	character	heard	really
accommodate	coming	immediately	receive
accumulate	committee	indispensable	recommend
acquaint	correspondence	inoculate	resistance
across	cough	instead	rhythm
address	course	irresistible	says
agreeable	definitely	knew	scene
a lot (*not* alot)	describe	knowledge	secretary
all right (*not* alright)	disappear	library	separate
almost	disappoint	lightning	since
always	doctor	maintenance	speech
among	doesn't	meant	straight
another	dropped	minute	studying
appreciate	embarrass	necessary	success
asked	enough	noticeable	supersede
athletic	every	occasion	surely
beautiful	exception	occurred	surprise
before	excitement	occurrence	though
believe	exhilarate	often	thought
benefit	experience	omitted	threw
boundary	feasible	once	together
break	February	piece	toward
broccoli	foreign	pleasant	until
built	friend	principal [of school]	weird
business	grammar	privilege	which
captain	handkerchief	probably	woman
certain	having	realize	writing

ACTIVITY 6 _____

Find the misspelled words on the following sign. On the lines provided below the sign, write each misspelled word correctly.

> Hikers and Campers:
>
> Please acquaint yourself with the following park rules:
>
> 1. Keep the trail beutiful—don't litter.
> 2. Stay within the marked boundries.
> 3. Seperate campfires from brush with dirt and stones.
> 4. No writeing on boulders or carving on trees.
> 5. Report any dangerous occurences to the park ranger.
> 6. Appoint a group leader, and stick tagether.
> 7. Do not leave behind forein materials (trash, food scraps).
>
> Thanks for comeing. Have a pleasent time!

1. _____
2. _____
3. _____
4. _____
5. _____

6. _____
7. _____
8. _____
9. _____
10. _____

Spelling Difficult Words

Everyone has his or her own spelling demons. Did you spot any of yours in the list on page 95? You may be interested to know that by simply writing a challenging word correctly, you help train your brain to remember the correct sequence of letters.

Get a stack of **ten** index cards. On one side of each card, write a word that you often misspell. Choose words from the list in this book, or select others. Now take it a step farther. Write each word repeatedly, as many times as it will fit on one side of the index card. As you write, think about memory aids that will help you remember how to spell the word. Finally, flip over each card and use the word in a sentence.

Words Often Confused

In addition to words that are tricky to spell, English has its share of words that are easily—and often—confused. Note the correct spelling of the words in boldface type.

We will **accept** all applications **except** those submitted after the deadline.

In middle school, I was taller **than** Petre. **Then** he had a growth spurt.

Jessica can sing beautifully, but she is **too** shy **to** go onstage.

During study hall, Mr. Noyse was **quite** happy that we were so **quiet**.

Bettina, when did you **lose** the tooth that was **loose**?

Patrick asked **whether** Jorge liked Michigan's snowy **weather**.

It's cute how the puppy chases **its** tail.

If **you're** coming over, please bring **your** football.

They're preparing for **their** performance over **there**.

Where do you plan to **wear** that tuxedo, Andre?

ACTIVITY 7

In each sentence, underline the correct spelling.

> **Sample:**
>
> I heard a noise, but nothing seemed to be (*there, their*).

1. Let's give the Rockettes a hand! They've put on (*quite, quiet*) a show.

2. Before cold (*whether, weather*) arrives, let's collect coats for the homeless shelter.

3. Juanita loves spicy foods; she says mild foods are (*to, too*) forgettable.

4. Congratulations! I heard that (*your, you're*) sculpture won an award at the show.

5. Truthfully, it's insensitive of you not to (*accept, except*) my apology.

6. The jeans were too (*lose, loose*); as a result, they hung low on his hips.

7. First I heard a siren, (*than, then*) I saw the flashing lights.

8. (*It's, Its*) ridiculous to obsess about your weight, don't you think?

9. When Tio got (*they're, there, their*), play rehearsals had started without him.

10. Pauline vows never to (*where, wear*) plaid.

11. Did anybody (*lose, loose*) a camera at the zoo?

12. Meet me at the amphitheater, in front of (*it's, its*) south entrance.

13. (*Where, Wear*) is my contact lens case?

14. I've traveled to every one of the United States (*accept, except*) Alaska.

15. The thief was (*quite, quiet*), but motion sensors detected him anyway.

16. (*Your, You're*) kidding!

17. Wow! Hal can type faster (*than, then*) anyone else I've ever seen.

18. (*They're, There, Their*) first kiss was short but heartfelt.

19. Do you know (*whether, weather*) Ms. Li is offering extra credit in biology?

20. I was addressing the package (*to, too*) Granny, but I couldn't remember her zip code.

Writing Application

Using the Dictionary to Aid Spelling

In addition to studying the ten sets of challenging words on page 97, become familiar with the differences in meaning and spelling in the words in the following list. With your teacher's approval, work with **two** classmates to divide the list into thirds—eight word sets apiece.

On a separate sheet of paper, write each of your words and a brief definition of it. Then, use each word correctly in a sentence. Whenever you need help, use a dictionary. Finally, exchange papers and proofread your classmate's work, checking for correct spelling and usage of each word. Correct any errors you find.

advice, advise	complement, compliment
affect, effect	council, counsel
aisle, isle	decent, descent, dissent
already, all ready	desert, dessert
altar, alter	hole, whole
altogether, all together	passed, past
a while, awhile	peace, piece
brake, break	principal, principle
breath, breathe	somebody, some body
capital, capitol	waist, waste
chose, choose	weak, week
coarse, course	whose, who's

Abbreviations and Numbers

Use the following helpful guidelines for spelling and using abbreviations and numbers.

GUIDELINE	EXAMPLES
Titles Place titles such as *Mr., Ms., Mrs., Dr.,* and *Prof.* before a proper name. Place designations such as *M.D.* and *Ph.D.* after a comma following the name.	*Mr.* Denzel Washington, *Ms.* Tyra Banks, *Dr.* Carl Sagan M. H. Abrams, *Ph.D.* Laura Thomas, M.D.
Streets, States, etc. In a sentence, do not abbreviate the names of streets, states, countries, continents, days of the week, months, or units of measure.	It happened on Lincoln *Street* near the deli. We'll study on *Monday* at the library. This steak weighs eight *ounces.*
Addresses For postal addresses, use proper abbreviations for states and street designations. For a complete list of abbreviations, go to the U.S. Postal Service's Web site, at www.usps.com and do a search for "abbreviations."	Drive = Dr. Road = Rd. Street = St. Boulevard = Blvd. California = CA Florida = FL Texas = TX New York = NY
Volume, Chapter, Page In sentences, write out the words *volume, chapter,* and *page.* When writing a source citation or bibliography, use the appropriate abbreviation (*vol. or vols., ch. or chs., p. or pp.*). *Note:* For exact format of citations and bibliographies, consult the style guide recommended by your teacher.	In Chapter Two, the author explains the results of her "splendiferous experiment" (Johnson, 2004, p. 56). Johnson, Nelda. *Experiments in Science.* Vol. 2. New York: Science House, 2004.
Acronyms Do not use periods with initials (*SAT, NATO, NASA, UNICEF, AIDS*). If your reader may not know what the initials stand for, spell out the words in the first instance of use, and place the initials in parentheses, as shown at right. Then use the initials after that.	Thousands of students will take the *SAT* this weekend. Opponents of the *North American Free Trade Agreement (NAFTA)* met yesterday in Chicago. Special speakers on *NAFTA* issues include Dr. Jerome Gerard.
Years When using B.C. or A.D. with a year, place B.C. after the year. Place A.D. before the year.	3500 B.C. A.D. 2005
Numbers When you use numbers in sentences, write out the number if it can be expressed in one or two words. Use figures for other numbers **unless** the number is the first word in a sentence. Always spell out a number that begins a sentence.	I invited *twenty-five* friends to the party, but only *seventeen* showed up. At the pet-adoption event, *111* dogs and cats found loving homes. *One hundred eleven* dogs and cats found loving homes at the pet-adoption event.

11 Review of Using Grammar and Mechanics

To review specific guidelines for using grammar and mechanics correctly in sentences, you can turn to the following pages in this book:

(a) Using *verbs:* page 70

(b) Using *nouns:* page 39

(c) Using *modifiers:* page 71

(d) Using *pronouns:* page 71

(e) Using *punctuation:* pages 77–78

(f) Using *capitalization:* page 84

(g) Using *spelling:* page 90

ACTIVITY 1 _____

In the following passage, there is one error in grammar or mechanics in each sentence. Cross out each error and, when needed, write a correction above it.

Many teens in America looks forward to their sixteenth birthday, when they finally can get their driver's license. Others look forward too turning twenty-one—and legal. But how many teens look forward to there eighteenth birthday? At this age: true power is bestowed upon a young person. Now, he or she are eligible to vote.

Before claiming that new power, however, the Individual must first register to vote. Convenient, many public places make voter-registration cards available. Look for cards in a libary, at the DMV (Department of Motor Vehicles), or at Armed Forces recruitment centers. internet users can download a mail-in form. In a search engine, just type "mail-in voter registration application" and your states name. Be sure to register to vote in you're state of residence.

When election times come around, twenty-first-century young people may have wondered if they can vote on the Internet. That option, unfortunate for Web fans, is not yet available. Instead; registered voters must go to a polling place. They're is a variety of types of polling places. Most are assigned based on where a person live. Libraries schools, and

churches are common polling places. A park or a beach are a possibility, too. At the polling

place, someone checks your name on the list of registered voter's and gives you a ballot.

At this point; your task is simple: Vote!

ACTIVITY 2 _____

Use the clues to unscramble each word in the titles of famous works of literature. Then write the titles—using correct punctuation and capitalization—on the lines provided.

> **Sample:**
>
> EAIARCM   HET   UELFAIUBT
>
> _____"America the Beautiful"_____
>
> *This song is often mistaken for the American national anthem.*

1. NMILAA   AMRF

_____

In this novel by George Orwell, animals can talk.

2. INALNAOT   RPGIECHGAO

_____

This magazine is known for its gorgeous photographs.

3. ETH   ANRVE

_____

This is a poem by Poe about a bird who knows one word.

4. TEH   ULEB   THELO

_____

Stephen Crane wrote this short story about a place to stay.

5. A   EDMMMSRIU   'SNTHIG   EDMRA

_____

In this Shakespeare play, fairies meddle in humans' love lives.

In the following poem, numbered blanks show where words have been left out. Look at the item that corresponds with each blank and circle the letter of the best choice to fill the blank.

When We Two Parted
George Gordon, Lord Byron

When __(1)__ two parted
   In silence and tears,
Half broken-hearted
   __(2)__ sever for years,
Pale grew thy cheek and cold,
   __(3)__ thy kiss;
__(4)__ that hour foretold
   Sorrow to this.

The dew of the morning
   __(5)__ chill on my brow—
It felt like the warning
   Of what I __(6)__ now.
Thy vows are all broken,
   And light is thy __(7)__
I hear thy name __(8)__,
   And share in its shame.

They name thee before __(9)__,
   A knell to mine ear;
A shudder comes __(10)__ me—
   Why wert thou so dear?
They know not I knew thee,
   Who knew thee __(11)__ well:—
Long, long shall I rue thee,
   Too __(12)__ to tell.

In secret we met—
   In silence I __(13)__,
That thy heart could forget,
   Thy spirit __(14)__.
If I should meet thee

1. **A.** us
   B. we
   C. ourselves

2. **D.** To
   E. Too
   F. Two

3. **A.** Cold
   B. Colder
   C. Coldest

4. **D.** Truely
   E. Truley
   F. Truly

5. **A.** Sinked
   B. Sunked
   C. Sunk

6. **D.** feel
   E. feels
   F. felt

7. **A.** fame."
   B. fame;
   C. fame'

8. **D.** speak
   E. spoke
   F. spoken

9. **A.** me
   B. myself
   C. I

10. **D.** oer'
    E. oe'r
    F. o'er

After long __(15)__

How should I greet thee?——

With silence and tears.

11. A. to
    B. too
    C. two

12. D. deep
    E. deeper
    F. deeply

13. A. greive
    B. grieve
    C. greeve

14. D. deceive
    E. decieve
    F. deceeve

15. A. years,
    B. years:
    C. years,"

ACTIVITY 4

Use the poem in Activity 3 to answer the following questions.

1. How would you punctuate the poem's title in an essay about the poem? Write the title with correct punctuation.

   _____

2. The first stanza ends with the pronoun *this.* At first you may wonder what *this* refers to—"This *what*?" Think about the stanza and then write a noun to specify what *this* refers to.

   this _____

3. In stanza 1, Byron uses the archaic pronoun *thy.* What modern pronoun could properly replace *thy*?

   _____

4. In stanza 3, Byron uses the archaic pronoun *thou.* What modern pronoun could properly replace *thou*?

   _____

5. In stanza 4, Byron uses the archaic pronoun *thee.* What modern pronoun could properly replace *thee*?

   _____

6. In stanza 3, Byron uses an apostrophe to form an unusual contraction. Why do you think he does this?

   _____

   _____

7. In stanza 2, why does Byron use *its* instead of *it's*?

_____

8. Which rule for using the comma best fits how it is used in stanza 1? (You can look back at the table of comma rules on page 77.)

_____

9. Using your knowledge of why we use marks of punctuation, analyze Byron's use of the dash (—) in the poem. What do you believe is the purpose of the dash? Write a rule for using the dash and give an example from the poem to illustrate your rule.

_____

_____

_____

10. Analyze Byron's use of capital letters in the poem by answering these two questions:

(a) What are two rules of capitalization that Byron follows? (You can look back at the chart of capitalization rules on page 84.)

_____

_____

(b) How does Byron use capitalization in a way that the rules in this book don't address? Write a rule to address this use of capital letters.

_____

Writing
Application

Using Grammar and Mechanics

What do you think is—or was—the relationship between the speaker in Byron's poem and the person to whom the words are spoken? How do you explain the ideas expressed by "silence," "tears," "secret," and "deceive"?

On a separate sheet of paper, write **three** paragraphs of at least five sentences each, explaining your interpretation of the poem. Answer the questions above and include references to other specific parts or words in the poem. In your response, use at least one direct quote from the poem. Finally, check your work for correct use of grammar and mechanics.

Using Grammar and Mechanics

It's time to take a break from traditional grammar exercises. The following activities ask you to explore how people use grammar and mechanics in the real world, outside your classroom walls. Which activity sparks your interest? Choose an activity to complete; then, with your teacher's approval, share the results with your classmates. Have a good time!

I Don't Know Nothing!

Double negatives are a no-no in English, but is this true of other languages? Find out what role double negatives play, if any, in another language. For example, are they used at all? Are they used in informal, but not formal, speech? Or perhaps they are not a grammar error at all. To support your findings, prepare a list of example sentences using double negatives in your chosen language and then translate the sentences into English.

Yellow

Clifton Fadiman, a book editor and radio quiz-show host, once quipped, "The adjective is the banana peel of the parts of speech." Based on your experience reading books and other print materials, how would you explain this metaphor? Use examples of adjectives in sentences to support your explanation.

The Power of a Letter

Have a little fun with your favorite magazines. Grab a pile of them at a library or in your own room, and take a look at the cover headlines. Now, play around with the spellings of words to form funny versions of what's printed. Add suffixes, prefixes, or individual letters, or swap out letters. For example, a cover story on "Pretty Hair" becomes "Pretty Hairy." "Romantic First-Kiss Stories" becomes "Romantic Fast-Kiss Stories." Turn your new headlines into a comedy routine, or make a mock-up of a magazine cover showcasing your humor.

A Face as Round as a Froot Loop

Modifiers play a delightful role in similes. A simile is a comparison of two unlike things that uses the word *like, as,* or *than.* Talented speechwriters, great talk-show hosts, unforgettable poets, charming new friends—all these people and more use adjectives and adverbs in similes to express compelling comparisons. Try creating unforgettable similes by brainstorming 15 or 20 of them. Then type up a list of your top ten.

Man Bites Dog

How do newspapers use verb tense to draw in readers, not to mention inform them of facts? Do a study of verb tense in newspapers. For example, when a headline shows tense, what tense is it usually? Is the article itself in the same tense? What about subtitles within articles? What conclusions can you draw from the ways newspapers use verb tense?

Montessori Method

The Montessori method of educating young children uses hands-on, personalized ways of connecting children with key concepts such as numbers, shapes, subtraction, etc. For example, to teach vowels, a Montessori teacher may cut out the shapes of vowels in differently textured materials—a sandpaper *A,* a felt *E,* a carpet-scrap *I,* you get the idea. Use your imagination to prepare a Montessori-style lesson on punctuation for eight-year-olds. Include basic rules for using the five types of punctuation in Lesson 8.

Capitalize This!

How important is capitalization to a printed event program? Think of the kinds of information included in the program for a play, an awards banquet, a wedding, or another event. Choose an event that interests you and create a one-page program for it (either a real event or one that you create in your imagination). Make the program as informative as possible and notice how capitalization helps you communicate to your readers. Notice if you use capitalization in ways not covered in Lesson 9 (all caps, for example). If you had to create the same program without any capitalization, what would you have to do differently?

The Book of Erica

To make the possessive forms of nouns in English, the apostrophe is crucial. In contrast, other languages show possession without the apostrophe. How do they do this? Prepare a list of phrases or sentences in English, each of which uses the possessive form of a noun. Then translate each sentence into a language that does not use the apostrophe. Finally, write a *literal* translation of the sentence back into English and compare the differences in the English versions.

Using Grammar and Mechanics

Directions: Look at the item with the same number as the underlined part. Circle the letter of the best replacement for the underlined portion and write it on the blank. If the current portion is best, choose the letter for *NO CHANGE*.

political correctness
1

Let's face it. Political correctness undermines a person's ability to express

themselves truthfully. Since when do we ignore the
2
right to free speech granted us by the Constitution? Nowadays, you have to watch your words, rein in your opinions, and pretend to be just like everyone else. People today
is afraid of difference. Political correctness is just a way
3
to make everyone think

alike, speak alike, and act alike. I, for one, am tired of it.
4

When I walked down the halls of my school, I see
5
students of every height, shape, color, and income level. I say it like it is.

That there guy is fat. That foreign girl needs to learn
6
English better. That group of kids should stop acting like they're being persecuted for the color of their skin.
Have I offended you? Maybe. But now do you know my true thoughts and what kind of person I am? Sure you do! And you know what? it's okay if you disagree
7
with me. That's my point! We should all have the freedom to say what we think instead of using preselected phrases like

"senior citizen" instead of "old lady" or "homeless person" instead of "bum."
8
Think about how you would express yourself if you

_____ **1. A.** NO CHANGE
 B. Political correctness
 C. Political Correctness
 D. political Correctness

_____ **2. F.** NO CHANGE
 G. theirself
 H. himself
 J. him or herself

_____ **3. A.** NO CHANGE
 B. was
 C. are
 D. were

_____ **4. F.** NO CHANGE
 G. think alike; speak alike;
 H. think alike speak alike
 J. think alike: speak alike:

_____ **5. A.** NO CHANGE
 B. walk
 C. walking
 D. have walked

_____ **6. F.** NO CHANGE
 G. This here
 H. That
 J. That their

_____ **7. A.** NO CHANGE
 B. It's
 C. Its
 D. its

_____ **8. F.** NO CHANGE
 G. "senior citizen" instead of "old lady" or "homeless person" instead of "bum".

H. "senior citizen instead of old lady" or "homeless person instead of bum."

J. "senior citizen instead of old lady or homeless person instead of bum."

<u>didn't</u> have to worry about the PC police. What would
9
you say differently? Do you even know what your own opinions are, or have you been too afraid to explore them? Nowadays it's easy to take the easy way

<u>out</u> to hold the majority opinion. You may
10

<u>think,</u> why have an original point of view if people are
11
going to get offended when I express it?

   Once we are willing to cut straight to the truth about other people, we are better prepared to do the same for

<u>ourselfs.</u> Are you hiding behind some PC label yourself?
12
Maybe you come from an economically challenged family. Why not just say

<u>your'e</u> poor. What's the big deal? Lots of other people
13
are, too. Maybe being poor wouldn't have such a stigma if people weren't afraid to say the word out loud.

   And so, dear reader, here is a homework assignment for you. For one week, express yourself as I do—
<u>free and honest.</u> See what happens. See how people
14
respond. You'll learn

<u>alot</u> about the people around you—and even more about
15
yourself.

9. A. NO CHANGE
B. did'nt
C. didnt'
D. didn't not

10. F. NO CHANGE
G. out:
H. out;
J. out"

11. A. NO CHANGE
B. thinking
C. thought
D. have thunk

12. F. NO CHANGE
G. ourself
H. ourselves
J. ourselve

13. A. NO CHANGE
B. youre
C. your
D. you're

14. F. NO CHANGE
G. freely and honest
H. free and honestly
J. freely and honestly

15. A. NO CHANGE
B. a lot
C. allot
D. a lots

PART II _____

Directions: In each item, certain words are underlined and labeled. Circle the letter of the underlined part that contains an error. If the item has no error, circle *E* for *No error*.

_____ **16.** The film _Girl with a Pearl Earring_ stars Scarlett Johansson and is about the
                              A   **B**

dutch painter Jan Vermeer. No error
C   **D**   **E**

_____ **17.** I can't hardly read this note you wrote because your handwriting is too messy.
         A   **B**   **C**   **D**

No error
E

_____ **18.** One of the eggs were cracked accidentally during the drive home from the
                              A   **B**

supermarket; I'm not sure whether I should throw it out. No error
C   **D**   **E**

_____ **19.** With you and me in starting positions, the competition at Friday's game will be
                              A   **B**   **C**

fierce. No error
D   **E**

_____ **20.** Robert Frost, famous for poems such as "Stopping by Woods on a Snowy
                                                            A

Evening" once wrote, "A poem begins in delight and ends in wisdom." No error
B   **C**   **D**   **E**

_____ **21.** A Grammy Award is given by the Recording Academy to honor artistic or technical
            A   **B**

achievement, not necessarily sales or standing in the charts. No error
C   **D**   **E**

_____ **22.** Leprosy, also called Hansen's disease, is caused by a bacterium it is treatable
         A   **B**   **C**

but not curable. No error
         D   **E**

_____ **23.** Two friends walked into a self-service laundry; one turned to the other and says, "Did
            A   **B**   **C**

you hear the one about the flying cow?" No error
                              D   **E**

_____ **24.** I should tell you one thing: The seedless grapes are more fresher than the
                              A   **B**

strawberries this week, at least in my opinion. No error
C   **D**   **E**

_____ **25.** During our trip to the southwest, we were amazed by the prairies of Texas, the
                              A   **B**   **C**

rocky cliffs of New Mexico, and the deserts of Arizona. No error
                    D   **E**

3 Phrases and Clauses

In Part One of this book, you reviewed the eight parts of speech, and in Part Two you learned useful rules and guidelines for using grammar and mechanics in sentences. Now we come to Part Three, which will teach you to identify phrases and clauses and to use them correctly in sentences.

A **phrase** is simply a sequence of words that are related grammatically, and that does not have a subject and/or a predicate. A phrase can come at the beginning, middle, or end of a sentence.

PHRASES: *Working quickly*, Fritz finished the puzzle.

Who is your friend *with the spiky hair*?

My first task is *to type my book report*.

In Lessons 12 and 13, you will learn about specific types of phrases, including **prepositional phrases** and **verbal phrases**.

Knowing how to recognize phrases and their uses in sentences will be helpful when you learn about clauses. Besides that, any time you write, your ability to use phrases correctly will strengthen your sentences and add clarity and conciseness to them.

A **clause** is a related sequence of words that has a subject and a predicate. A **main clause** can stand alone as a sentence, but a **subordinate clause** is dependent on a main clause to form a complete sentence. Being able to recognize clauses and their uses will help you write clear, complete sentences.

With a good understanding of phrases and clauses, you will excel at writing the four kinds of sentences correctly. The final section of this book, Part Four, covers the four sentence types. For now, let's begin your study of phrases.

12 The Prepositional Phrase

A *phrase* is a word group used as a single part of speech. Its purpose is to add detail to a sentence. This lesson explains the prepositional phrase and how it is used in sentences.

As you recall, a *preposition* is a word that relates its object to another word in the sentence.

The documentary *about sharks* intrigued me.
PREP.   OBJ.

Commonly Used Prepositions

about	along	along with	around	behind	beneath	beside	between	by
down	for	from	in	in front of	inside	instead of	near	next to
on	out	outside	through	to	under	until	with	without

 A *prepositional phrase* is made up of a preposition, its object, and any modifiers of that object.

Please arrive *on time*.
PREP. OBJ.

A friend *from my old neighborhood* stopped by.
PREP.   OBJ.

In just a minute, I'll start the movie.
PREP.   OBJ.

As you can see in the examples above, a prepositional phrase may be placed at the beginning, middle, or end of a sentence, depending on the sentence.

ACTIVITY 1

Underline the prepositional phrase or phrases in each sentence.

> **Samples:**
>
> **a.** Are you going to the Cher concert this evening?
>
> **b.** No, I'm going to a movie or to a baseball game.

1. At a concert, the seats near the stage cost more, and those in the back cost less.

2. At a movie theater, however, all seats cost the same.

3. Movies with big-name stars in them may sell out quickly.

4. Therefore, getting in line early for your ticket is a good idea.

5. Then you can grab a snack from the concession stand and get to your seat on time.

An object of a preposition may be compound.

The flag *with* *stars and stripes* is the American flag.
COMPOUND OBJ.

My piggy bank is full *of* *nickels, dimes, and quarters*.
COMPOUND OBJ.

ACTIVITY 2

On each blank, write a prepositional phrase with a compound object. Refer to the list of prepositions on page 112, or use other prepositions.

Samples:

a. *On the desk and floor* are stacks of library books.

b. A comet *with a bright light and long tail* passed overhead last night.

1. Orange paint spilled _on my dog and cat_ .

2. _On the benches and grass_ rested a dozen exhausted athletes.

3. Hilda looks great in the shirt _with pink and blue dots_ .

4. That sporty car _____ belongs to Jasper.

5. My dresser drawers are full _____ .

Adjective Phrases

A prepositional phrase may be used as an *adjective* to modify a noun or pronoun.

A prepositional phrase that modifies a noun or a pronoun is called an *adjective phrase*. It tells *which one(s)* or *what kind*.

The person *with the most points* is the winner.

(Which person? The person *with the most points*.)

New fashion designs *in silk and linen* were featured in the show.

(What kind of designs? Designs *in silk and linen*.)

ACTIVITY 3

Underline the adjective phrase in each sentence. Then draw an arrow from the phrase to the noun or pronoun it modifies.

Samples:

a. *Bend It Like Beckham* is a feel-good movie about soccer.

b. An application packet from my first-choice college arrived today.

1. Every weekend, I enjoy the comics section of the Sunday newspaper.

2. Give me the one without mayonnaise, please.

3. "The books inside this glass case are very rare and valuable," said the librarian.

4. Someone with great artistic skill painted this colorful mural.

5. The Shakespeare Outdoors Festival is presenting a performance in the park.

Two or more adjective phrases may modify the same word.

A collection *of seashells* or *of river rocks* would brighten this windowsill.

The gift *of flowers from my boyfriend* was sweet.

An adjective phrase may modify the object in another prepositional phrase.

Mr. Canton was happy *with your performance on the math exam*.

ACTIVITY 4

Underline each adjective phrase. Then draw an arrow from the phrase to the noun or pronoun it modifies.

> **Samples:**
>
> **a.** Each morning, birds <u>on the shore</u> and <u>across the lake</u> sang cheerily.
>
> **b.** Someone <u>with a contact</u> <u>on the inside</u> is the most likely culprit.

1. Anything in stripes or with polka dots does not flatter my figure.

2. Runoff from the factory up the river has contaminated the water supply.

3. A quick trip on a bus or by subway will take you there.

4. Everyone on the men's and women's basketball teams at my school stands six feet tall or taller.

5. A smile on my friend's face for no reason makes me glad I know him.

Writing Application

Using Adjective Phrases

On a separate sheet of paper, write **five** sentences, using at least one adjective phrase in each sentence. Remember, adjective phrases tell *which one(s)* or *what kind* about a noun or pronoun.

Then, with your teacher's approval, exchange sentences with a classmate. Underline each adjective phrase in your classmate's sentences and draw an arrow to the noun or pronoun it modifies. Share the results with each other.

Adverb Phrases

A prepositional phrase may be used as an *adverb* to modify a verb, an adjective, or an adverb.

 A prepositional phrase that modifies a verb, an adjective, or an adverb is called an *adverb phrase*. Adverb phrases tell *when, where, why, how,* or *to what extent.*

Madison was impressive *in today's game*. (Impressive when? *in today's game*)
ADJ.

The soccer ball flew *past the goalie*. (The ball flew where? *past the goalie*)
VERB

Madison is a star *because of her talent*. (She is a star why? *because of her talent*)
VERB

Madison kicks the ball *with precision*. (Kicks how? *with precision*)
VERB

Madison runs faster *than her sister*. (Faster to what extent? *faster than her sister*)
ADV.

ACTIVITY 5

Underline the adverb phrase or phrases in each step. Then draw an arrow from each phrase to the word or word group it modifies. Two sentences have hints in parentheses.

> **Samples:**
>
> **a.** A piñata is not just for kids.
>
> **b.** Actually, a piñata party is fun for teens and for adults, too.

How to Make a Simple Piñata

Part I

1. Fill a balloon with air and tie a knot in the neck. *(Fill how? Tie where?)*

2. Place some school glue in a shallow bowl and rip newspapers into narrow six-inch strips. *(Place where? Rip how?)*

3. Dip strips into the glue, then wrap them around the balloon.

4. The project should dry for several hours or overnight. Then repeat steps 3 and 4.

5. The hard part is over. The remaining steps will be inspirational to your creative side.

QUESTION: Does an adverb phrase always follow the word it modifies?

ANSWER: Not always. An adverb phrase that modifies a verb may sometimes come before the verb in the sentence.

Our class president spoke *at the assembly*.

At the assembly, our class president spoke.

Our class president stood *on the stage*.

On the stage stood our class president.

ACTIVITY 6

Underline the adverb phrase or phrases in each sentence. Then, draw an arrow from the phrase to the word or word group it modifies.

> **Samples:**
>
> **a.** The piñata must be completely dry for the remaining steps.
>
> **b.** Get an adult's help if you are under age sixteen.

How to Make a Simple Piñata

Part II

6. From the piñata's top, cut a two-inch circle. On either side, poke a small hole.

7. Thread string into one small hole and out the other. (You'll use this string later to hang the piñata.)

8. The decorating steps are easy enough for anyone.

9. Decorate the piñata with paint, tissue paper, or other materials.

10. Next, fill the piñata with wrapped candy or tiny gifts.

11. Get the circle you cut out of the top and tape it over the hole.

12. Decorate the circular piece with the same materials.

13. Using the string you inserted earlier, hang the piñata from a tree branch or another sturdy place.

14. Now your creation must be broken open with a broomstick.

15. With your friends, make this part into a fun game.

Revise each sentence, placing the adverb phrase in a different place in the sentence. If the adverb phrase comes *after* the verb, place the phrase *before* the verb in your revision. If the adverb phrase comes *before* the verb, place the phrase *after* the verb. Write your sentences on the lines provided.

Samples:

a. My mom will drive us home after the dance.

   After the dance, my mom will drive us home.

b. Across the rink skated Jared, the hockey team captain.

   Jared, the hockey team captain, skated across the rink.

1. One wilted rose was among the fresh ones.

   _____

2. Out of the airplane jumped a paratrooper.

   _____

3. Since yesterday, I have changed my mind.

   _____

4. Carmen's little brother was restless during the recital.

   _____

5. Without you, the entire evening was boring.

   _____

Composition Hint

You can strengthen your sentences and paragraphs by using prepositional phrases. For instance, choppy sentences can be combined by putting information into phrases.

CHOPPY: He researched mad cow disease. It was for his article. It added vital detail.

REVISED: His research *on mad cow disease* added vital detail *to his article*.

The example above uses an adjective phrase and an adverb phrase. Can you tell which is which?

Rewrite each set of choppy sentences as one strong sentence. Use adjective and/or adverb phrases to combine the sentences. Write on the lines provided.

Samples:

a. One fell. She is a trapeze artist. She landed. A safety net was there.

One of the trapeze artists fell and landed in a safety net.

b. A dancer showed off. She was on the dance floor. She had amazing moves.

On the dance floor, a dancer with amazing moves showed off.

1. The agent sold me a bus ticket. He was at the ticket counter. The ticket is to Philadelphia.

_____

2. Let's order a pizza. It will have pepperoni and thin crust. It will come from Luigi's.

_____

3. Fans were there. They sat in the stands. They were from the third baseman's hometown.

_____

4. Hilary's story was published. It was about a chess champion. It was published in a magazine.

_____

5. The minivan skidded. It went over the curb. Everything happened near the corner.

_____

ACTIVITY 9

There are over 20 one-word prepositions hidden in the puzzle, spelled forward, backward, up, down, or diagonal. Two are circled to help get you started. Find and circle 15 other prepositions.

   Then, on the lines that follow the puzzle, write 15 sentences. In seven sentences, use any seven of the prepositions to write adjective phrases. In eight sentences, use the other eight prepositions to write adverb phrases. Underline each prepositional phrase.

```
            E C N I S
          E D Y T H R O U G H
        R F O F E R D Y F C W A          E T
      P O C V D J X N J N Y M E L C      D L P
    A F Y ■ T S N I A G A P D X O T R    I E V G
    H E S D T B Q H V J C O Q I C S Z F O S K S S N
    N B K E R U J E B N Z U G N C E G K P N S Y P E I
    D O W N A F B P S W T S E U B P A L I F N S I R R
    O R Z W B L I H S J E N X E T S N O    L T C U
    A R O U N D  I R W R B Z H G E H       E K D
      E T W Y D K T V M W I N M U          U G
        I E N E W I T H O U T
        K B T D G P M H D
          R E Q A V
```

Adjective Phrases

1. _____

2. _____

3. _____

4. _____

5. _____

6. _____

7. _____

Adverb Phrases

8. _____

9. _____

10. _____

11. _____

12. _____

13. _____

14. _____

15. _____

Troublesome Preposition Pairs

Some prepositions are harder to use correctly than others. The prepositions in the following pairs are commonly confused with each other. Learn the correct use of each preposition in these pairs.

by/until

- Use *by* to show that an action will happen at or before a certain time in the future.

The package will arrive <u>*by Friday.*</u> (NOT *until Friday*)

- Use *until* to show that an action is ongoing up to a certain time in the future.

Each day, Manuel works <u>*until five o'clock.*</u> (NOT *by five o'clock*)

besides/except

- Use *besides* to express the idea of "with" or "plus." This preposition shows that something is included.

<u>*Besides Irma,*</u> *Osvaldo and Leno will be at the party.* (NOT *except Irma*)

- Use *except* to express the idea of "without" or "minus." This preposition shows that something is not included.

Irma arrived <u>*without her boyfriend.*</u> (NOT *besides her boyfriend*)

in/on

- Use *in* to express the idea of "inside."

Maria placed the groceries <u>*in the car.*</u> (NOT *on the car*)

- Use *on* to show that something is on the surface or top of something else.

Drops of rain fell <u>*on the car.*</u> (NOT *in the car*)

ACTIVITY 10

In each sentence, underline the correct preposition in parentheses.

> **Sample:**
>
> (<u>*Except,*</u> *Besides*) Roma, I like everyone in my English class.

1. Dad is gone on a business trip (*by, until*) next Wednesday.

2. Please put the papers (*in, on*) the envelope and mail it.

3. At dinner, Eva ate salad and bread (*except, besides*) some chicken.

4. Your book report must be turned in (*by, until*) this afternoon.

5. The kids are working a jigsaw puzzle (*in, on*) the table.

Write sentences that follow the instructions below.

> **Sample:**
>
> Use *until* to show that an action is ongoing up to a certain time.
>
> _You cannot drive until your sixteenth birthday._

1. Use *by* to show that an action will happen at or before a certain time.

_____

2. Use *besides* to show that something is included.

_____

3. Use *except* to show that something is not included.

_____

4. Use *in* to express the idea of "inside."

_____

5. Use *on* to show that something is on the surface or top of something else.

_____

13 The Verbal Phrase

The **verbal** gets its name from the word *verb* because verbals are formed from verbs. However, a verbal is not used as a verb. Instead, a verbal is used as a noun, an adjective, or an adverb.

NOUN: *Cheating* is forbidden.

              (*Cheating* is the subject of the sentence. It is formed from the verb *cheat*.)

              He was arrested for *stealing*.

              (*Stealing* is the object of a preposition. It is formed from the verb *steal*.)

ADJECTIVE: A *cracked* sidewalk led to the house.

              (*Cracked* modifies the noun *sidewalk*. It is formed from the verb *crack*.)

              Do these *faded* jeans look okay?

              (*Faded* modifies the noun *jeans*. It is formed from the verb *fade*.)

ADVERB: *To pass,* you must study.

              (*To pass* modifies the verb *must study*. It is formed from the verb *pass*.)

              Rasha was slow *to forgive*.

              (*To forgive* modifies the adjective *slow*. It is formed from the verb *forgive*.)

ACTIVITY 1

Practice recognizing verbals. Decide whether each underlined word or word group is used as a verb or as a verbal. Write *verb* or *verbal* on the line provided.

    Remember, a *verb* expresses action or a state of being. A *verbal* is used as a noun, an adjective, or an adverb—not as a verb.

Samples:

a. _____verbal_____ I am happy <u>to help</u>.

b. _____verb_____ Please <u>help</u> Aaron.

a. _____verb_____ Krista <u>is singing</u> a solo.

b. _____verbal_____ Are you shy about <u>singing</u>?

1. _____verbal_____ **a.** Do you want <u>to eat</u>?

   _____verb_____ **b.** Freddy <u>eats</u> too many snacks.

2. _____verb_____ **a.** My sister <u>is jogging</u> on the track.

   _____verbal_____ **b.** <u>Jogging</u> is my hobby.

3. _____verb_____ **a.** This plate <u>has been broken</u>.

   _____verbal_____ **b.** A <u>broken</u> plate is useless.

4. _____verbal_____   **a.** All <u>completed</u> entry forms go in this box.

   _____verb_____   **b.** <u>Have</u> you <u>completed</u> your entry form?

5. _____verbal_____   **a.** The <u>sleeping</u> puppy is cute.

   _____verb_____   **b.** Roger <u>is sleeping</u> late today.

6. _____   **a.** Monica arrived too quietly <u>to notice</u>.

   _____   **b.** I <u>noticed</u> your new hairdo.

7. _____   **a.** Julia <u>is knitting</u> a gorgeous sweater.

   _____   **b.** In my opinion, <u>knitting</u> can be relaxing.

8. _____   **a.** Janine was too angry <u>to speak</u>.

   _____   **b.** She <u>did</u> not <u>speak</u> to me again.

9. _____   **a.** Do you want some <u>fried</u> chicken?

   _____   **b.** It <u>was fried</u> in vegetable oil.

10. _____   **a.** Oops, I <u>erred</u> in my calculations.

   _____   **b.** <u>To err</u> is human.

The three kinds of verbals have specific names: *gerunds, participles,* and *infinitives.* A **verbal phrase** is made up of a verbal and its modifiers and/or complements. In the remainder of this lesson, we will look at each kind of verbal phrase separately.

Gerund Phrases

A verbal used as a noun is called a *gerund.* Recall these examples from the beginning of this lesson:

Cheating is forbidden.

He was arrested for *stealing.*

In these sentences, *cheating* and *stealing* are used as nouns. They are gerunds.

 A *gerund* is a verb form used as a noun in a sentence. A gerund ends in *ing*.

Sometimes, a gerund has an object, a modifier, and/or a complement. It is used together with these other words as a phrase. This group of related words is called a *gerund phrase.*

 A *gerund phrase* is made up of a gerund and its objects, modifiers, and/or complements. It is used as a noun in a sentence.

GERUND PHRASES: *Cheating on exams* is forbidden.

(*Cheating on exams* is used as the subject of the sentence.)

He was arrested for *stealing a car*.

(*Stealing a car* is used as the object of the preposition *for*.)

The professor observed *Hank's cheating*.

(*Hank's cheating* is used as the direct object of the verb *observed*.)

Notice that a verbal's use in the sentence determines whether it is part of a gerund phrase or a verb phrase. Compare the following examples of verb phrases to the examples of gerund phrases above.

VERB PHRASES: Several students *were cheating* on exams.

(*Were cheating* is the action performed by the subject *students*.)

Stop! That man *is stealing* a car!

(*Is stealing* is the action performed by the subject *man*.)

Hank *was cheating* on his history test.

(*Was cheating* is the action performed by the subject *Hank*.)

ACTIVITY 2

In each sentence, circle the gerund. Then underline the gerund phrase.

Samples:

a. Cleaning the filthy garage is not my idea of a good time.

b. I don't want to hear any more excuses about your being late!

1. Tuning this piano will take some time.

2. Helen, I apologize for yelling so loudly.

3. Please give owning a snake a chance.

4. One option is restoring an old car.

5. Everyone loves your singing.

6. One day, visiting the moon will seem commonplace, don't you think?

7. On the agenda for today is cleaning this entire city park.

8. Fran considered joining the debate team, but she joined the yearbook staff instead.

9. Dionne's bicycle riding is the highlight of every weekend.

10. Yesterday my neighbors were fined for not paying their taxes.

This activity has two parts, as follows.

Part I

Six of the eight verbs listed below can be placed in the grid to complete the interlocking pattern. Complete the puzzle by writing words forward, backward, up, or down. Two letters are inserted in the grid as clues.

suppose	believe	press	exhaust
stand	brush	shuffle	exhibit

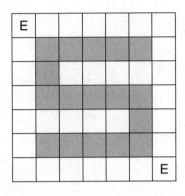

Part II

As you know, a gerund is the *ing* form of a verb. On the lines below, write sentences using each verb in the puzzle **as a gerund in a gerund phrase**. Underline each gerund phrase.

1. _____

2. _____

3. _____

4. _____

5. _____

6. _____

Participial Phrases

You may recall from Lesson 3 that a verb has four principal parts. For example, here are the principal parts of *laugh* and *choose*.

BASE FORM	PRESENT PARTICIPLE	PAST	PAST PARTICIPLE
laugh	(is) laughing	laughed	(has) laughed
choose	(is) choosing	chose	(has) chosen

In the examples above, notice the *present participle* and *past participle* forms. The participle forms of a verb may be used as adjectives in sentences.

A *participle* is a verb form that may be used as part of a verb phrase or as an adjective.

In Lesson 3, you learned about participles used as verbs. In this lesson, we focus on participles used as adjectives. Here are some examples.

Laughing, the woman pointed. (*Laughing* modifies *woman.*)

Only a *chosen* few were invited. (*Chosen* modifies *few.*)

A *cracked* sidewalk led to the house. (*Cracked* modifies *sidewalk.*)

Faded, the jeans look better. (*Faded* modifies *jeans.*)

Sometimes, a participle has an object, a modifier, and/or a complement. This group of related words is called a *participial phrase.*

 A *participial phrase* is made up of a participle and any objects, modifiers, and/or complements. It is used as an adjective in a sentence.

PARTICIPIAL PHRASES: The woman *laughing at you* is Rhonda.

Only a few, *chosen for their creativity,* were invited.

Cracked by age, the sidewalk leads to my house.

Faded by the sun, the jeans look great.

ACTIVITY 4

In each sentence, underline the participial phrase. Then draw an arrow from the phrase to the noun or pronoun it modifies.

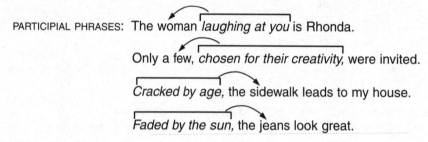

Samples:

a. In the ancient world, certain structures <u>constructed by men</u> were famous.

b. <u>Called the Seven Wonders of the World</u>, they were popular tourist destinations.

1. Included in world tours, these wonders delighted wealthy travelers.

2. The Egyptian pyramids, built between 2650 and 2500 B.C., are a marvel.

3. Still standing, they are the only wonder you can see today.

4. The Hanging Gardens of Babylon, known for their beauty, were also on the list of wonders.

5. Erected at Olympia, the statue of Olympian Zeus was sculpted of ivory and gold.

6. At Ephesus, the temple of Artemis, completed around 430 B.C., took 120 years to construct.

7. Artemis, called Diana by the Romans, was the Greek goddess of the hunt and nature.

8. Designed in honor of King Mausolus of Caria, the Mausoleum at Halicarnassus marked the king's burial site.

9. Estimated at 105 feet high, the Colossus of Rhodes was a huge bronze statue.

10. A white-marble lighthouse known as the Pharos of Alexandria stood on an Egyptian island.

Composition Hint

You can strengthen your sentences and paragraphs by using participial phrases. For instance, choppy sentences can be combined by putting information into phrases.

CHOPPY: He was tired of homework. He took a nap.

REVISED: *Tired of homework,* he took a nap.

Information in repetitive sentences can be streamlined by using phrases to form one concise sentence.

REPETITIVE: Jane photographed giraffes. The giraffes were nibbling green leaves.

REVISED: Jane photographed giraffes *nibbling green leaves.*

ACTIVITY 5

Revise choppy or repetitive sentences into one strong sentence by using one or more participial phrases. Write on the lines provided.

> **Samples:**
>
> **a.** These chairs were made by Grandpa. They are heirlooms.
>
>   _____Made by Grandpa, these chairs are heirlooms._____
>
> **b.** Regular passengers became acquainted. They were riding the train.
>
>   _____Riding the train, regular passengers became acquainted._____

1. This kitchen tool is called a whisk. It can whip up eggs.

   _____

2. Those girls are my friends. They are sitting by the pool.

   _____

3. Mr. Jarred turned to page 100. He read the class a poem.

   _____

4. The rare plant was frozen in ice. It was perfectly preserved.

   _____

5. The trophy was glazed in gold. It was given to the winner.

   _____

Infinitive Phrases

The third kind of verbal is the *infinitive.*

 An *infinitive* is a verb form that can be used as a noun, an adjective, or an adverb. Most infinitives begin with *to,* as in *to forgive.*

NOUNS: My dream is *to sing.* (*To sing* is a subject complement. It identifies the subject *dream.*)

Everyone wanted *to play.* (*To play* is the direct object of the verb *wanted.*)

ADJECTIVES: A fun song *to sing* is "Hello, Dolly." (*To sing* modifies *song.*)

The ones *to play* were Josh, Vinny, and Nan. (*To play* modifies *ones.*)

ADVERBS: *To pass,* you must study. (*To pass* modifies *must study.*)

Rasha was slow *to forgive.* (*To forgive* modifies *slow.*)

ACTIVITY 6

Underline the infinitive in each sentence.

> **Samples:**
>
> **a.** The printer <u>to use</u> is marked with a number 1.
>
> **b.** Is everyone ready <u>to go</u>?

1. The birthday gifts to wrap are sitting over there.

2. Ivan speaks Russian too fast to understand.

3. To deceive is despicable.

4. Do you need directions to follow?

5. Those to invite are the juniors and seniors.

Sometimes an infinitive has an object, a modifier, and/or a complement. This group of related words is called an *infinitive phrase.*

 An *infinitive phrase* is made up of an infinitive and any objects, modifiers, or complements. The phrase is used as a noun, an adjective, or an adverb in a sentence.

NOUNS: My dream is *to sing on Broadway.*

Everyone wanted *to play the lead role.*

ADJECTIVES: A fun song *to sing to your girlfriend* is "Hello, Dolly."

The ones *to play main characters* were Josh, Vinny, and Nan.

ADVERBS: *To pass the test,* you must study.

Rasha was slow *to forgive my offense*.

Remember, an infinitive phrase always includes *to* plus a *verb*. This fact will help you distinguish between infinitive phrases and prepositional phrases beginning with the preposition *to*. As you know, a prepositional phrase is made up of a preposition and a *noun* or *pronoun,* never a verb.

INFINITIVE PHRASE: Fareed decided *to learn Japanese*.

(*To* is used with the verb *learn* to form the infinitive phrase. Even though *Japanese* is a noun, it follows the verb *learn;* this verb signals the phrase is an infinitive phrase.)

PREPOSITIONAL PHRASE: One day, he would travel *to beautiful Japan*.

(*To* is used with the noun *Japan* to form the prepositional phrase. A prepositional phrase never contains a verb.)

ACTIVITY 7

Underline the infinitives and infinitive phrases in the passage (there is a total of ten). Not every sentence contains an infinitive or infinitive phrase.

Samples:

a. Many young people want <u>to make a difference in their world</u>.

b. Often, however, they feel too inexperienced <u>to make a difference</u>.

Each day in our communities, homeless individuals try to find food and shelter. Whether you see them or not, they are out there, attempting to scratch out an existence. But solving the problems of the homeless is a job best left to adults, right? Think again. It shouldn't be that easy for a teen to dismiss the situation.

While it is true that adults fill influential roles such as mayor, police chief, and social worker, there are other roles to pursue. They include volunteer, activist, and problem solver. Around the country, many teens seek out ways to assist those in need. They search the Internet to find local shelters and relief organizations. They ask teachers and librarians to direct them to volunteer opportunities. They work in soup kitchens, they volunteer to staff donation drives, and they ask friends to donate clothing and food. Those who try to make a difference *do* make a difference.

Using Infinitive Phrases

On a separate sheet of paper, write **ten** sentences, each one using an **infinitive phrase**. Check your work to make sure you haven't accidentally used a prepositional phrase instead of an infinitive phrase.

With your teacher's approval, exchange sentences with a classmate. Underline each infinitive phrase in your classmate's sentences. Share the results with each other. If you had trouble identifying an infinitive phrase in a sentence, discuss this sentence with your classmate or teacher.

ESL Focus

Gerund and Infinitive Phrases after Verbs

A gerund or infinitive phrase may follow a verb.

Tariq <u>enjoys</u> repairing clocks. (gerund phrase)

Tariq <u>wants</u> to repair this clock. (infinitive phrase)

Certain verbs are usually followed by gerund phrases (not infinitive phrases). These verbs include *appreciate, avoid, consider, delay, discuss, enjoy, finish, mention, mind, postpone,* and *suggest.*

Khadeeja <u>considered</u> buying a computer.

Emmett <u>did</u> not <u>mind</u> missing the quiz.

Certain verbs are usually followed by infinitive phrases (not gerund phrases). These verbs include *agree, appear, ask, decide, expect, intend, need, plan, pretend, promise, refuse,* and *want.*

My little brother <u>asked</u> to go with us.

What <u>do</u> you <u>intend</u> to do now?

ACTIVITY 8

In each sentence, underline the correct word or word group in parentheses.

> **Samples:**
>
> **a.** Let's discuss (<u>*working*</u>, *to work*) on the science assignment together.
>
> **b.** I'm sorry, but I already promised (*working*, <u>*to work*</u>) with Keiko.

1. You should avoid (*chewing*, *to chew*) with your mouth open.

2. How wonderful! I did not expect (*seeing*, *to see*) you here.

3. Did Iliana finish (*mopping*, *to mop*) the floor in the break room?

4. The governor has agreed (*speaking*, *to speak*) at our graduation ceremony.

---

5. I was late because I needed (*buying, to buy*) gas on the way here.

6. Why is Fatima refusing (*coming, to come*) to breakfast?

7. Please consider (*coming, to come*) with me to the party on Friday.

8. Keenan suggested (*using, to use*) the Sunday comics as fun gift wrap.

9. Ricardo had been planning (*asking, to ask*) Melinda to the sports banquet.

10. We must act soon, so don't delay (*making, to make*) your decision.

14 Main and Subordinate Clauses

A *clause* is a word group that contains both a subject and its verb. In the following clauses, each subject is underlined once, and each verb is underlined twice.

CLAUSES: Ten <u>race cars</u> <u><u>zoomed</u></u> around the track.

Fans <u><u>were screaming</u></u> enthusiastically.

when two <u>cars</u> <u><u>collided</u></u>

because a <u>driver</u> <u><u>had taken</u></u> a risk

There are two kinds of clauses: those that *can* stand alone as a sentence and those that *cannot*. Look at the four examples above. The first two clauses can stand alone as sentences. The second two cannot.

 A *main clause* (also called an *independent clause*) expresses a complete thought and can stand alone as a sentence.

MAIN CLAUSES: <u>Rescuers</u> <u><u>rushed</u></u> to the accident.

Luckily, both <u>drivers</u> <u><u>were</u></u> unharmed.

 A *subordinate clause* (also called a *dependent clause*) does not express a complete thought and cannot stand alone as a sentence.

SUBORDINATE CLAUSES: as soon as the <u>cars</u> <u><u>collided</u></u>

if <u>he</u> <u><u>wants</u></u> to race again

ACTIVITY 1 _____

Each item below is punctuated as a complete sentence. However, only some items are complete sentences (main clauses); others are subordinate clauses. Decide which is which. On the blank, write *M* for *main clause* or *S* for *subordinate clause*.

Samples:

___M___ **a.** What do you value most in a relationship?

___S___ **b.** Since beauty is only skin deep.

_____ **1.** In my opinion, some people focus on looks too much.

_____ **2.** When I was going through puberty?

_____ **3.** Because that special someone will see beyond mere looks.

_____ **4.** Some of the nicest people are not the most attractive.

_____ **5.** Likewise, some attractive people are indeed unlikable.

_____ **6.** Before you make a decision based on appearance.

_____ **7.** Whether the person, not the outer package, is compatible with you.

_____ **8.** Besides, you may find a new friend.

_____ **9.** Where you least expect to find one.

_____ **10.** Just stay open to possibilities, no matter their appearance.

The Main Clause

As you know, a main clause contains both a subject and its verb.

I <u>am going</u> to the farmers' market.

Where <u>did</u> I <u>leave</u> my keys?

<u>Help</u> me to fix this flat tire. (The understood *you* is the subject.)

QUESTION: Does every sentence contain a main clause?

ANSWER: Yes. Every complete sentence is made up of at least one main clause.

QUESTION: Can a sentence contain more than one main clause?

ANSWER: Yes. A sentence may contain multiple main clauses. The clauses must be properly joined. One way to join clauses is with a comma and a conjunction. A semicolon can also join main clauses.

       main clause   main clause

I <u>am going</u> to the farmers' market, *but* <u>one</u> of the car tires <u>is</u> flat.

       main clause   main clause

<u>Help</u> me to fix this flat tire; <u>it will take</u> only a minute.

ACTIVITY 2 _____

Underline each main clause. Do not underline a conjunction that joins main clauses.

> **Samples:**
>
> **a.** <u>Have you ever completed a triathlon?</u>
>
> **b.** <u>You may be inspired by Rudy Garcia-Tolson</u>, for <u>he has run many</u>.

1. Rudy Garcia-Tolson is just a regular teenager, except for one thing.

2. Both of his legs are amputated below the knee.

3. Even with this disability, Rudy is a triathlete, and he is a hero to many.

4. As a ten-year-old, he ran his first triathlon.

5. After that race, he was hooked.

6. Many people were doubtful; they were unaware of Rudy's abilities.

7. At first, there were no races for double amputees, but now there are.

8. Rudy has helped to change people's attitudes and expectations.

9. In addition, he is a spokesperson for the Challenged Athletes Foundation.

10. He lives in Bloomington, California, and he encourages other disabled young people to become athletes.

The Subordinate Clause

As you know, a subordinate clause contains a subject and its verb, but the clause cannot stand alone as a complete sentence.

QUESTION: Why can't a subordinate clause stand alone as a sentence?

ANSWER: A subordinate clause does not express a complete thought; therefore, it cannot stand alone as a sentence.

SUBORDINATE CLAUSES: since Randy is meeting Ursula there

which was a surprise to me

whom Paulette invited to the dance

To express a complete thought, a subordinate clause must be joined to a main clause.

subordinate clause   main clause

Since Randy is meeting Ursula there, he needs the car.

main clause   subordinate clause

Ursula danced with real flair, which was a surprise to me.

main clause   subordinate clause

I like Ryan, whom Paulette invited to the dance.

ACTIVITY 3

Use each of the following subordinate clauses in a complete sentence. To do so, join each subordinate clause to a main clause that you make up. Write your sentences on the lines provided.

Samples:

a. while you wait

Please have a seat while you wait.

b. who is my best friend

I went to a movie with Olivia, who is my best friend.

1. when I looked out the window

_____

2. because Luling does not like broccoli

_____

3. that I want to buy

_____

4. who was standing beside my locker

_____

5. before you go

_____

QUESTION: How can I recognize a subordinate clause?

ANSWER: First, identify the main clause of the sentence. Then look for any additional word groups that contain both a subject and its verb. The key difference is that a main clause can stand as a complete sentence, but a subordinate clause cannot.

main clause   subordinate clause

I will eat *whatever you are having.*

main clause   subordinate clause

The artist is proud of these songs *that she herself wrote.*

QUESTION: Where does a subordinate clause belong in a sentence?

ANSWER: A subordinate clause can come before, after, or in the middle of a main clause.

Until school starts again, I will work during the day.

This is the CD *that I bought online.*

Sarah gave FooFoo, *who is her poodle,* a shampoo.

QUESTION: Can a sentence contain more than one subordinate clause?

ANSWER: Yes. A sentence can contain multiple subordinate clauses.

subordinate clause   subordinate clause

Although Mike means well, he is annoying *when he tells those stupid jokes.*

sub. clause   sub. clause

Sarika keeps her earrings in this tray *that she made* *while she was at camp.*

Underline each subordinate clause. If two subordinate clauses are written back-to-back, underline each one separately.

Samples:

a. Let me tell you about a lesson <u>that I learned the hard way</u>.

b. A small party was <u>what I had in mind</u> <u>when I called a few friends</u>.

1. One day last summer I invited a few friends over so we could have a party.

2. Those whom I invited showed up with snacks that they had bought.

3. We had a great time until Jessica called Todd, who was her new boyfriend.

4. Todd came over, bringing five of his friends even though they were not invited.

5. Before I knew it, some of those guys had called kids that I had never met.

6. After they made those calls, even more people showed up.

7. By eight o'clock, a hundred people, who were all strangers, had packed into my backyard.

8. Whatever I did, I could not get these party crashers to leave.

9. Indoors, people trashed the living room and broke a vase that was very valuable.

10. Desperate, I called the cops and asked that they end this party for me.

Composition Hint

In your writing, make sure you do not punctuate a subordinate clause as a complete sentence. Doing so creates a *sentence fragment*.

I sat down next to Lalaine. <u>Although I barely know her.</u>
SENTENCE FRAGMENT

<u>I sat down next to Lalaine, although I barely know her.</u>
COMPLETE SENTENCE

Decide whether each item contains a sentence fragment. If it does, make changes directly to the item to correct the error. If the item is already correct, write *C* for correct on the blank.

Samples:

_____ **a.** The security guards were surprised ~~How~~ at h that thief escaped their notice.

___C___ **b.** All swim-team members should arrive early to the meet that we have on Friday.

_____ 1. Chris and his buddies enjoyed their volleyball game. Until it started raining.

_____ 2. I don't care where we go or what we do. Whatever you want. It's fine.

_____ 3. Before I added salt, these beans tasted bland. What do you think?

_____ 4. My report is on Hemingway, who was a brilliant American writer.

_____ 5. Bridget will take the car to school today. Unless you need it, Kelsey.

_____ 6. After the airplane lands. That is when you can unfasten your seat belt.

_____ 7. Let's invite the new girl to sit at the empty desk that is behind you.

_____ 8. Whichever college you choose. You'll get a great education at any of them.

_____ 9. Does anyone know? Whether the tryouts are canceled due to rain?

_____ 10. My job in the mall is fun because I can see my friends and make new friends while they shop in my store.

Uses of Subordinate Clauses

In a sentence, a subordinate clause may be used as a noun, an adjective, or an adverb.

 A *noun clause* is used as a subject or as an object in a sentence.

SUBJECTS: *Whoever prepared this meal* has my gratitude.

Which fork you use does not matter.

Truthfully, *why he did it* is a mystery.

OBJECTS: Tell me about *what happened.* (object of the preposition *about*)

Hanna asked *whose the cat was.* (direct object of the verb *asked*)

Razina gave *whoever asked* her honest opinion. (indirect object of the verb *gave*)

A noun clause is usually introduced by one of these words:

how	where	whoever
that	whether	whom
what	which	whomever
whatever	whichever	whose
when	who	why

Underline the noun clause in each sentence.

> **Samples:**
>
> **a.** <u>How that lizard escaped its terrarium</u> is quite a story.
>
> **b.** After <u>what happened</u>, I am afraid of heights.

1. You can do this research paper on whatever interests you most.

2. Do you know whose notebook this is?

3. Everyone is wondering when you are coming back to school.

4. Why this fire started is the park ranger's main concern.

5. Please tell me that you have a backup disk.

6. Can you tell which is which?

7. Unfortunately, I don't know whether I can afford basketball camp.

8. Draw me a map of where I should go.

9. Gleefully, Brodie tossed water balloons at whoever wasn't looking.

10. Whoever finds your class ring will surely put it in lost-and-found.

 Writing Application

Using Noun Clauses

Choose **ten** words from the list of words that typically introduce noun clauses (page 137). Use them to write **ten** sentences, each one containing a noun clause.

With your teacher's approval, exchange sentences with a classmate. Underline each noun clause in your classmate's sentences. If you have trouble identifying a noun clause in a sentence, consult with your classmate or your teacher. Finally, share the results with your classmate.

 An *adjective clause* is used to modify a noun or pronoun.

The person *whom I admire most* is my grandmother.

Those *whose cars are parked in the fire lane* should move them.

The milk *that you are drinking* expired yesterday.

An adjective clause usually begins with a relative pronoun. The relative pronouns are these: *who, whom, whose, which,* and *that.*

ACTIVITY 7

Underline the adjective clause in each sentence. Then draw an arrow from the clause to the noun or pronoun it modifies.

> **Samples:**
>
> **a.** That which does not destroy us makes us stronger.
>
> **b.** Actually, Vikesh, whom I met at a coffee shop, is a dental hygienist.

1. This pineapple-upside-down cake, which I made myself, is for the bake sale.

2. Most applicants whom we hire are available to work weekends.

3. Wow! The Web site that you created has gotten a lot of traffic.

4. The woman who needs your babysitting services is Mrs. Gomez.

5. A few whose artwork was chosen were invited to an artists' workshop.

Composition Hint

When you use *who* in a subordinate clause, make sure it works as the *subject* of the clause. When you use *whom,* make sure it works as an *object* in the clause. In the examples below, each subordinate clause is underlined.

SUBJECT: Give your money to Tabitha, *who* is collecting dues.

(*Who* functions as the subject of the verb *is.* The entire clause modifies *Tabitha.*)

OBJECT: Tabitha is the officer to *whom* you should pay your dues.

(*Whom* functions as the object of the preposition *to.* The entire clause modifies *officer.*)

Tabitha, *whom* we elected unanimously, is our treasurer.

(*Whom* functions as the direct object of the verb *elected.* The entire clause modifies *Tabitha.*)

ACTIVITY 8

Complete each adjective clause below by writing *who* or *whom* on the blank. Then underline the entire clause and draw an arrow from it to the word it modifies.

> **Samples:**
>
> **a.** I have a photograph signed by Butterfly McQueen, __whom__ I met in Hollywood once.
>
> **b.** Butterfly, __who__ played Prissy in *Gone With the Wind*, enjoyed a long career in acting.

1. Clark Gable, _____ moviegoers adored, played Rhett Butler in *Gone With the Wind*.

2. Scarlett O'Hara was played by Vivien Leigh, for _____ I created a fan page on the Web.

3. David O. Selznick, _____ produced the film, received a star on Hollywood's Walk of Fame in October 2004.

4. The woman to _____ everyone owes thanks is Margaret Mitchell.

5. Mitchell is the author _____ wrote the novel *Gone With the Wind*.

When an adjective clause is not essential to the meaning of the sentence, it is set off by commas. The commas show that you could remove the clause, and the sentence would still express its main idea.

NONESSENTIAL CLAUSES: Gustave Flaubert, *who was French,* wrote *Madame Bovary.*

Few Americans have been to Cuba, *which is south of Florida.*

When an adjective clause is essential to the meaning, it is not set off by commas.

ESSENTIAL CLAUSES: The athletes *whose grades fell* were not allowed to play.

I am allergic to anything *that has peanuts in it.*

QUESTION: How do I know whether an adjective clause is essential or nonessential?

ANSWER: Try reading the sentence without the clause. Does the sentence still express its main idea? Then the clause is probably nonessential and should be set off with commas. Does the sentence no longer express the same thought? Then the clause is necessary and should not be set off by commas.

Give it a try. Do you think the underlined clause in the following sentence is essential or nonessential?

Yams which taste like sweet potatoes are a popular Thanksgiving dish.

Without the clause, the sentence reads *Yams are a popular Thanksgiving dish.* This shortened sentence expresses the main idea of the original sentence. Therefore, the underlined clause is nonessential. It should be set off by commas.

Try it again. Read the following sentence.

Teachers who coach a sport earn a little extra.

Without the clause, the sentence reads *Teachers earn a little extra.* This version of the sentence is missing vital information. Only teachers *who coach a sport* earn a little extra. Therefore, the underlined clause is essential. It should not be set off with commas.

Often (but not always) a subordinate clause beginning with *that* is essential, while a subordinate clause beginning with *which* is nonessential.

ESSENTIAL: The rumor *that you spread* was false.

(This subordinate clause is essential, so it is *not* set off by commas.)

NONESSENTIAL: The rumor, *which was false*, was about Miguel and me.

(This subordinate clause is nonessential, so it *is* set off by commas.)

Underline the adjective clause in each sentence. If the clause is nonessential, insert a comma or commas to set it off. If the clause is essential, do not add commas.

> **Samples:**
>
> **a.** The job opening at the telephone company requires someone <u>who is bilingual</u>.
>
> **b.** Robert, <u>whom friends call Tank</u>, dreams of being a pro football player.
>
> **c.** Talitha collected homework assignments for Max, <u>whose leg was broken yesterday</u>.

1. Oprah Winfrey whom I met at a book signing is America's best-loved talk show host.

2. Dolphins which are related to whales have been trained to perform tricks.

3. The man whose dog was stolen has offered a reward for Alfie's safe return.

4. Edgar Allan Poe who was orphaned as a child had a fantastic imagination.

5. Eagerly I read my new e-mails which filled my Inbox.

6. The candidate whom voters elect will serve the public faithfully.

7. A black widow whose bite is poisonous should not be tampered with.

8. I need to talk to someone who won't judge me.

9. That is the nicest thing that anyone has ever said to me!

10. Consumers prefer toothpaste that has a minty flavor.

A subordinate clause may be used as an adverb.

 An *adverb clause* modifies a verb, an adjective, or an adverb.

EXAMPLES: <u>Before I left</u>, I grabbed an apple. (adverb phrase modifying a verb)

This movie is longer <u>than I expected</u>. (adverb phrase modifying an adjective)

Carmen danced as gracefully <u>as her instructor dances</u>. (adverb phrase modifying an adverb)

An adverb clause is introduced by a *subordinating conjunction*. Commonly used subordinating conjunctions are these:

after	if	until
although	since	when
as	so that	where
because	than	whether
before	unless	while

ACTIVITY 10

Underline the adverb clause in each sentence.

> **Samples:**
>
> **a.** Lightning struck that tree <u>before it fell across the road</u>.
>
> **b.** <u>So that everyone is safe</u>, workers must wear hard hats in this area.

1. Dara arrived at the softball field as the men's team was leaving.

2. I'm donating this coat to the Salvation Army, unless you want it.

3. Clearly, Samima understands chemistry better than I do.

4. When you are finished in the kitchen, please clean up after yourself.

5. We are eating fish tonight whether you like it or not.

ACTIVITY 11

Use the word in parentheses to write an adverb clause to complete each sentence. Be sure to include a period or other end mark at the end of a sentence.

> **Samples:**
>
> **a.** *(although)* Here is the computer lab, _____although it is closed right now._____
>
> **b.** *(since)* _____Since these shorts are on sale_____ , I'll buy two pairs.

1. *(because)* Orson's friends laughed _____

2. *(if)* _____ , you will be fired.

3. *(after)* What did Zandy's boyfriend say _____

4. *(while)* _____ , I'll go get the popcorn.

5. *(where)* Blackbeard looked for his treasure _____

QUESTION: How do I punctuate an adverb clause in a sentence?

ANSWER: Follow these three guidelines.

(a) An introductory adverb clause is usually followed by a comma.

Until the bell rings, please read quietly in your seats.

Because I felt so happy, I did a little dance.

(b) An adverb clause at the end of a sentence is not usually preceded by a comma.

Please read quietly in your seats *until the bell rings*.

I did a little dance *because I felt so happy*.

(c) If an adverb clause at the end of a sentence does not affect the meaning of the sentence, then a comma may precede it.

Sandee agreed to the plan**,** *although she had doubts about it.*

We can ride there with my mom**,** *unless you have a better idea.*

Writing Application

Punctuating Adverb Clauses

Consult the list of subordinating conjunctions on page 141. On a separate sheet of paper, use five different conjunctions to write **five** adverb clauses. With your teacher's approval, exchange papers with a classmate.

Now, write **five** complete sentences using the adverb clauses you've been given. Be sure to use proper punctuation.

When you have finished, discuss the results with your classmate. Do you both agree on the usage of commas? If not, discuss why.

15 Using Phrases and Clauses as Modifiers

As you learned in Lessons 12–14, phrases and clauses may be used as modifiers (adjectives or adverbs) in sentences.

MODIFYING PHRASES: A stranger *standing across the room* smiled at me. (adjective phrase)

Where is the equipment *to be repaired?* (adjective phrase)

Dance tryouts will be held *in the gymnasium.* (adverb phrase)

MODIFYING CLAUSES: A stranger *who stood across the room* smiled at me. (adjective clause)

Before you get angry, listen to my explanation. (adverb clause)

You look older *since you grew a beard.* (adverb clause)

ACTIVITY 1

Underline each modifying phrase or clause. Draw an arrow from the modifier to the word or word group it modifies.

Samples:

a. Determined to catch a white whale, Captain Ahab is the main

character in *Moby-Dick.*

b. One animal that stands clearly in my memory is the White Rabbit.

1. "Casey at the Bat," written by Ernest L. Thayer, tells about a baseball player.

2. In an Arabian tale, Ali Baba opens a cave of gold by saying a magic password.

3. Bram Bones is the man who becomes a rival to Ichabod Crane.

4. Both men are trying to win the love of beautiful Katrina.

5. Published in 1818, *Frankenstein* is a famous tale of a doctor who creates a monster.

6. Rapunzel, who is a fairy tale character, is known for her long, long hair.

7. Don Quixote, accompanied by Sancho Panza, goes on many escapades.

8. The character whom I like most is Beowulf, who slew a monster.

9. This rabbit is a character in the much-loved *Alice's Adventures in Wonderland.*

10. Whether you believe it or not, Rumpelstiltskin could spin straw into gold.

Misplaced Modifiers

Misunderstanding can sometimes occur when a modifier is not placed next to the word or word group it modifies.

 A *misplaced modifier* is a modifier that is placed too far away from the word it modifies, creating an awkward or confusing sentence.

MISPLACED: *Drizzled with chocolate sauce,* Curtis thought the berries were delicious.

(Is Curtis drizzled with chocolate sauce?)

CLEAR: Curtis thought the berries *drizzled with chocolate sauce* were delicious.

(The phrase clearly modifies *berries*.)

MISPLACED: I recited the poem to my English teacher *that I like the most*.

(Does *that I like the most* modify *teacher* or *poem?*)

CLEAR: I recited the poem *that I like the most* to my English teacher.

(The clause clearly modifies *poem*.)

MISPLACED: Brenda decided to take a nap, *exhausted by soccer practice*.

(*Exhausted by soccer practice* seems to modify *nap*.)

CLEAR: *Exhausted by soccer practice*, Brenda decided to take a nap.

(The phrase clearly modifies *Brenda*.)

QUESTION: How can I tell if a modifier is misplaced?

ANSWER: Follow these steps.

1. Underline the modifier.
2. Draw an arrow to the nearest word it could modify.
3. Ask, "Does this modifier logically modify that word?"
4. If the answer is no, the modifier is probably misplaced.
5. If the answer is yes, the modifier is placed correctly.

ACTIVITY 2

Underline each modifier in the following sentences and draw an arrow from the modifier to the nearest word it could modify. If all modifiers in a sentence are placed correctly, write *C* for *correct* on the blank. If a modifier is misplaced, write *MM* for *misplaced modifier*.

Samples:

___MM___ **a.** Planted in front of the school, the view was brightened by flowers.

___C___ **b.** Swinging from vines, the chimp shrieked with delight.

_____ 1. Until the storm blows over, we can take shelter in that old cabin.

_____ 2. Go grab a dish towel in the kitchen hanging near the sink.

_____ 3. The turkey sandwich eased my hunger, which was made on rye bread.

_____ 4. My trophies, arranged on a shelf, remind me of the rewards of perseverance.

_____ 5. Darcy read about bodysurfing in the library.

_____ 6. Diving into the pool, Mavis swam toward the bottom of the deep end.

_____ 7. To find the video arcade, just ask any mall employee.

_____ 8. About extra credit, those whose grades are a D may talk to me.

_____ 9. Before you go to bed, please wind the cuckoo clock in the den.

_____ 10. Using art software, the images were easily created.

QUESTION: How do I revise a sentence to correct a misplaced modifier?

ANSWER: Place the modifier as close as possible to the word it modifies.

MISPLACED: *Covering two miles of hilly road,* I thought the race was too hard.

(This misplaced participial phrase modifies *I.*)

REVISED: I thought the race, *covering two miles of hilly road,* was too hard.

(Now the phrase properly modifies *race.*)

MISPLACED: I have a collection of CDs in my bedroom *in a CD tower.*

(This misplaced adverb phrase seems to modify *bedroom.*)

REVISED: I have a collection of CDs *in a CD tower* in my bedroom.

(Now the phrase properly modifies *collection.*)

ACTIVITY 3

On the lines below, rewrite each sentence from Activity 2 that contains a misplaced modifier. In your revision, place the modifier as close as possible to the word it modifies.

Sample:

(The following sample is a revision of Sample a in Activity 2.)

The view was brightened by flowers planted in front of the school.

1. _____

_____

_____

2. _____

_____

3. _____

_____

4. _____

_____

5. _____

_____

ACTIVITY 4 _____

Each sentence below contains a misplaced modifier. Rewrite each sentence, placing the modifier correctly.

> **Samples:**
>
> **a.** Trained in CPR, my friend's life was saved by a bystander.
>
> _My friend's life was saved by a bystander trained in CPR._
>
> **b.** Betty does bookkeeping for her clients, who is good at math.
>
> _Betty, who is good at math, does bookkeeping for her clients._

1. The children should not sit on the sofa covered with mud.

_____

_____

2. Buried in the sand, Vivian was delighted to find the ruby ring.

_____

_____

3. Someone dented my car door who parked next to me.

_____

_____

4. Conroy ordered the enchiladas for dinner with chili sauce.

_____

_____

5. Mr. Elke prepared us for a history test writing dates on the chalkboard.

_____

_____

Dangling Modifiers

A modifier should logically modify a word in the same sentence. If the modifier does not modify a word in the sentence, we say it is *dangling*.

 A *dangling modifier* does not clearly and logically modify a word or word group in the sentence.

DANGLING: *Sweeping the balcony,* a pot of flowers fell through the railing.

              (This phrase does not logically modify any word in the sentence.)

CLEAR: *Sweeping the balcony,* Grace knocked a pot of flowers through the railing.

              (In this revision, the phrase logically modifies *Grace.*)

DANGLING: The evening was a success, *entertained by great singing.*

              (This phrase does not logically modify any word in the sentence.)

CLEAR: The audience, *entertained by great singing,* thought the evening was a success.

              (In this revision, the phrase logically modifies *audience.*)

QUESTION: How can I tell if a sentence contains a dangling modifier?

ANSWER: First, use common sense. Often (but not always), you'll recognize a dangling modifier because the sentence seems incomplete, odd, or even ridiculous.

Another method of identifying a dangling modifier is this four-step process:

1. Underline each modifier in the sentence.
2. Locate the word each modifier modifies.
3. If you find the modified word, double-check that the modifier *logically* modifies it.
4. If you cannot locate a word logically modified, the modifier is probably dangling.

ACTIVITY 5

Underline each modifying phrase and clause in the following sentences. Draw an arrow from each modifier to the word or word group it *logically* modifies. If each modifier logically modifies a word, write *C* for *correct* on the blank. If a sentence has a dangling modifier, write *DM* for *dangling modifier*.

> **Samples:**
>
> __DM__ **a.** Terrified of heights, a ride on the Ferris wheel was out of the question.
>
> __C__ **b.** Fortified by vitamins and minerals, the cereal made a healthy breakfast.

_____ **1.** Wearing life vests, the boat trip should be safe.

_____ **2.** His grades in trigonometry improved, helped by his study partner.

_____ **3.** Hanging on the wall, the oriental rug was a lovely work of art.

_____ **4.** Passionate about gymnastics, every day is a new opportunity to practice.

_____ **5.** Standing in line for half an hour, we hoped the movie was worth the wait.

_____ **6.** I paid top dollar for this CD, released last week.

_____ **7.** Spoken softly, my friend's words were barely audible.

_____ **8.** Sunburned after a day at the lake, aloe vera gel would feel soothing.

_____ **9.** Keeping us safe from ultraviolet sunrays, ozone occurs in the upper atmosphere.

_____ **10.** Known for serving fattening, fried foods, the new healthy menu was a surprise.

QUESTION: How do I revise a sentence to correct a dangling modifier?

ANSWER: Add, remove, or replace words in the sentence so that the modifier logically modifies a word or word group.

DANGLING: *Running on empty,* Rupak needed to buy gasoline.

(This phrase does not logically modify any word in the sentence.)

CLEAR: *Running on empty,* Rupak's pickup needed gasoline.

(Now the phrase modifies *pickup*.)

CLEAR: Rupak needed to buy gasoline for his pickup, *which was running on empty.*

(In this slightly different version, the phrase has been rewritten as a clause to modify *pickup*.)

As you can see in the example above, revising a sentence with a dangling modifier may not be simple. You must add new words, and you may need to rearrange existing words.

When a modifier begins a sentence, make sure the word or word group it modifies comes directly after it. Add or rearrange words until the modifier is used logically.

DANGLING: *Although briefly caught in the net,* the escape came quickly.

(This phrase does not logically modify *escape*.)

DANGLING: *Although briefly caught in the net,* the fish's escape came quickly.

(The phrase is still dangling. Even though the word *fish's* makes clear that the escape was that of a fish, the phrase still modifies *escape*, not *fish*.)

CLEAR: *Although briefly caught in the net,* the fish escaped quickly.

(Now the phrase logically modifies *fish*.)

On the lines below, rewrite each sentence from Activity 5 that contains a dangling modifier. Add, remove, or replace words in the sentence so that the modifier logically modifies a word or word group.

> **Sample:**
>
> *(The following sample is a revision of Sample **a** in Activity 5.)*
>
> **a.** Terrified of heights, Pacey knew a ride on the Ferris wheel was out of the question.

1. _____

_____

2. _____

_____

3. _____

_____

4. _____

_____

5. _____

_____

ACTIVITY 7

Rewrite each sentence below to correct the dangling modifier.

> **Samples:**
>
> **a.** Using a cell phone all the time, that habit became too costly for me.
>
> Using a cell phone all the time, I realized the habit had become too costly.
>
> **b.** Blown way out of proportion, Mom was extremely upset with me.
>
> Mom was extremely upset with me for the mistake, which she blew way out of proportion.

1. Crowded with students between classes, I could barely push my way through.

_____

_____

2. Playing at the top of his form, the college scout was suitably impressed.

_____

_____

3. Usually spread with cream cheese, peanut butter is also an option.

_____

_____

4. With a glance to the audience, they seemed riveted to the stage.

_____

_____

5. Filled with remorse, a sincere apology was in order.

_____

_____

ACTIVITY 8

This activity has two parts, as follows.

Part I

Distribute the five letters accompanying each item—not necessarily in the order they appear—to form a compound noun or pronoun. Each word contains a total of nine letters.

Things You Might Find at the Beach

Sample:	R S N I O	S H O R E L I N E
1.	I F R O T	_ _ O _ P _ _ N T
2.	R I G L F	_ _ _ _ E _ U A _ D
3.	N E S U R	S _ _ _ _ C _ _ E N
4.	K B R O W	_ _ A _ D _ A L _
5.	E I S H M	_ O _ _ T _ _ N G
6.	B S R F O	_ U R _ _ _ _ A _ D
7.	U A E S H	_ _ N B _ T _ _ R
8.	R N O A D	S _ _ _ _ S T _ _ M
9.	D E E O R	_ V _ _ Y B _ _ Y
10.	A L L E E	S _ _ S H _ _ _ _ S

Part II

Now, write ten sentences on the following lines. In each sentence, use a phrase or clause to modify one of the ten words you created in Part I. Underline each modifying phrase and clause.

Sample:

Washed with clear blue water, the shoreline stretched before me.

11. _____

12. _____

13. _____

14. _____

15. _____

16. _____

17. _____

18. _____

19. _____

20. _____

16 Review of Phrases and Clauses

A *phrase* is a sequence of related words that does not contain both a subject and its verb. A phrase is used as a single part of speech. Specifically, an **adjective phrase** modifies a noun or a pronoun. An **adverb phrase** modifies a verb, an adjective, or an adverb. Different kinds of phrases exist.

- A prepositional phrase that modifies a noun or a pronoun is called an *adjective phrase*. It tells *which one(s)* or *what kind*.
- A prepositional phrase that modifies a verb, an adjective, or an adverb is called an *adverb phrase*. Adverb phrases tell *when, where, why, how,* or *to what extent*.
- A *gerund phrase* is made up of a gerund (a verb form used as a noun) and any objects, modifiers, and/or complements. It is used as a noun.
- A *participial phrase* is made up of a present or past participle verb form and any objects, modifiers, and/or complements. It is used as an adjective.
- An *infinitive phrase* is made up of an infinitive (*to* plus a verb) and any objects, modifiers, or complements. The phrase is used as a noun, an adjective, or an adverb.

For Activities 1 and 2, read the following excerpt from "Young Goodman Brown," a short story by Nathaniel Hawthorne. The story is set a few years before the Salem witch trials of 1692. Then answer the questions that follow.

from "Young Goodman Brown"
Nathaniel Hawthorne

Young Goodman Brown came forth at sunset into the street of Salem village; but put his
              (1)   (2)

head back, after crossing the threshold, to exchange a parting kiss with his young wife.
            (3)   (4)

And Faith, as the wife was aptly named, thrust her own pretty head into the street, letting

the wind play with the pink ribbons of her cap while she called to Goodman Brown.
         (5)   (6)

"Dearest heart," whispered she, softly and rather sadly, when her lips were close

to his ear, "prithee put off your journey until sunrise and sleep in your own bed tonight. A
 (7)

lone woman is troubled with such dreams and such thoughts that she's afeared of herself
         (8)   (9)

sometimes. Pray tarry with me this night, dear husband, of all nights in the year."

"My love and my Faith," replied young Goodman Brown, "of all nights in the year, this
              (10)

one night must I tarry away from thee. My journey, as thou callest it, forth and back again,
       (11)

must needs be done 'twixt now and sunrise. What, my sweet, pretty wife, dost thou doubt

me already, and we but three months married?"

ACTIVITY 1 _____

In the excerpt from "Young Goodman Brown" on page 153, certain parts are under-lined and numbered. Look at the item below that corresponds to each numbered part. Circle the letter of the best description of the underlined part. The first item is completed as a sample.

1. **A.** prepositional phrase used as an adjective

   B. participial phrase

   (C.) prepositional phrase used as an adverb

   D. infinitive phrase used as an adverb

2. **F.** infinitive phrase used as noun

   G. prepositional phrase used as an adverb

   H. gerund phrase

   J. prepositional phrase used as an adjective

3. **A.** participial phrase

   B. gerund phrase

   C. prepositional phrase used as an adverb

   D. prepositional phrase used as an adjective

4. **F.** infinitive phrase used as an adverb

   G. prepositional phrase used as an adverb

   H. participial phrase

   J. gerund phrase

5. **A.** prepositional phrase used as an adjective

   B. participial phrase

   C. prepositional phrase used as an adverb

   D. gerund phrase

6. **F.** prepositional phrase used as an adverb

   G. prepositional phrase used as an adjective

   H. participial phrase

   J. infinitive phrase used as an adverb

7. **A.** infinitive phrase used as an adverb

    B. gerund phrase

    C. prepositional phrase used as an adjective

    D. prepositional phrase used as an adverb

8. **F.** participial phrase

    G. prepositional phrase used as an adjective

    H. infinitive phrase used as an adverb

    J. prepositional phrase used as an adverb

9. **A.** gerund phrase

    B. prepositional phrase used as an adjective

    C. prepositional phrase used as an adverb

    D. participial phrase

10. **F.** prepositional phrase used as an adjective

    G. infinitive phrase used as a noun

    H. prepositional phrase used as an adverb

    J. participial phrase

11. **A.** prepositional phrase used as an adjective

    B. gerund phrase

    C. participial phrase

    D. prepositional phrase used as an adverb

ACTIVITY 2

**Use the excerpt from "Young Goodman Brown" to answer the questions that follow.
Write your answers on the lines provided.**

1. In the third paragraph, Hawthorne uses the prepositional phrase *'twixt now and sunrise.* The preposition *'twixt* is archaic (old and no longer used). Which modern-day preposition could be used instead of *'twixt* to form this phrase? _____

2. What word or word group does *'twixt now and sunrise* modify?

_____

3. The prepositional phrase *'twixt now and sunrise* is used as what part of speech?

_____

4. List three adverb phrases in the passage that are not underlined and numbered.

a. _____

b. _____

c. _____

5. Write one adjective phrase from the passage that is not underlined and numbered.

_____

6. What kind of phrase does Hawthorne use most in this passage—prepositional phrase, participial phrase, gerund phrase, or infinitive phrase?

_____

7. Why do you think Hawthorne uses a lot of this particular kind of phrase?

_____

_____

_____

Writing Application

Using Phrases

In the excerpt from "Young Goodman Brown," the husband does not clearly explain to his wife what he intends to do during the night. When she expresses uncertainty about his actions, he calls her trust in him into question.

When it comes to explaining one's actions, some people live by the motto, "What they don't know won't hurt them." Do you agree or disagree with this motto? Why? Have you ever withheld information from someone in order to protect him or her? If so, what were the circumstances? If not, would you consider doing so under certain circumstances?

On a separate sheet of paper, write **two** paragraphs in response to these questions. Use complete sentences and underline each phrase you use. Label each phrase *Prep.* for *prepositional phrase*, *Part.* for *participial phrase*, *Ger.* for *gerund phrase*, or *Inf.* for *infinitive phrase*. Make sure your paragraphs contain at least one example of each of the four phrase types listed here.

A *clause* is a sequence of related words that contains both a subject and its verb.

- A *main clause* expresses a complete thought and can stand alone as a sentence.
- A *subordinate clause* does not express a complete thought and cannot stand alone as a sentence.
- A *noun clause* is a subordinate clause used as a subject or as an object.
- An *adjective clause* is a subordinate clause used to modify a noun or pronoun.
- An *adverb clause* is a subordinate clause used to modify a verb, an adjective, or an adverb.

For Activities 3 and 4, read the following poem.

Ozymandias
Percy Bysshe Shelley

1 <u>I met a traveller from an antique land</u>
(1)

Who said: Two vast and trunkless legs of stone

Stand in the desert. . . . Near them, on the sand,

Half sunk, a shattered visage[1] lies, whose frown,

5 And wrinkled lip, and sneer of cold command,

Tell <u>that its sculptor well those passions read</u>
(2)

Which yet survive, stamped on these lifeless things,

The hand <u>that mocked them</u>, and the heart <u>that fed</u>:
(3)   (4)

And on the pedestal these words appear:

10 "My name is Ozymandias,[2] King of Kings:

<u>Look on my works, ye Mighty, and despair!"</u>
(5)

Nothing beside remains. Round the decay

Of that colossal wreck, boundless and bare

<u>The lone and level sands stretch far away</u>.
(6)

[1] *visage:* face

[2] *Ozymandias:* the Greek name for Ramses II of Egypt

ACTIVITY 3

In the poem, certain word groups are underlined and numbered. On the line below that corresponds to each number, write the best description of the underlined part. Select your answers from this list:

main clause   adverb clause

noun clause   adjective clause

One item is completed as a sample.

1. *main clause*

2. _____

3. _____

4. _____

5. _____

6. _____

ACTIVITY 4 _____

Use "Ozymandias" to answer the following questions.

1. Write three prepositional phrases that are used as adjectives in the poem.

    a. _____

    b. _____

    c. _____

2. Write three prepositional phrases that are used as adverbs in the poem.

    a. _____

    b. _____

    c. _____

3. In line 4, the verb form _shattered_ is used as what part of speech? _____

4. In line 5, the verb form _wrinkled_ is used as what part of speech? _____

5. In line 4, the phrase _Half sunk_ is used as what part of speech? _____

    Recall that a **_modifier_** is a word or word group that modifies, or describes, another word or word group. Modifiers are either adjectives or adverbs.
- A _misplaced modifier_ is placed too far away from the word it modifies, creating an awkward or confusing sentence.
- A _dangling modifier_ does not clearly and logically modify a word or word group in the sentence.

ACTIVITY 5 _____

Underline and label the misplaced and dangling modifiers in the following passage. Two modifiers are underlined and labeled as samples.

    misplaced
<u>Rising from the desert sand</u>, I could see the ruins from a mile away. When I got close, I

realized what they were. Lying half buried in the sand, a gigantic carved face stared up at

me. Unblinking in the bright sun, sand drifted across. Shaped like a solid box, I saw a chunk

of stone nearby. It was a pedestal. On top of it, two massive stone legs stood. Extending

high into the air, any viewer would be awed by the legs. Created long ago, I was over-

                             dangling
whelmed by what I saw. I moved closer, <u>drawing me to it.</u>

ACTIVITY 6

On the lines below, revise the passage in Activity 5, correcting the misplaced and dangling modifiers. The first and last sentences have been revised for you as examples.

I could see the ruins, rising from the desert sand, from a mile away.

_____

_____

_____

_____

_____

_____

_____

_____

_____

_____

_____

_____

_____

_____

_____

_____

_____

I moved closer, for the face was drawing me to it.

For each underlined word group, decide two things: (1) Is it a main clause, a subordinate clause, or a phrase? (2) If it is a subordinate clause or a phrase, is it used as a noun, an adjective, or an adverb? Write your answers on the lines provided.

Samples:

SENTENCE	MAIN CLAUSE, SUB. CLAUSE, OR PHRASE?	NOUN, ADJ., OR ADV.?
a. <u>I looked more closely at the carved face</u> that lay in the sand.	main	
b. Its expression seemed haughty, as if this king was used to <u>having his orders obeyed.</u>	sub	noun

SENTENCES	MAIN CLAUSE, SUB. CLAUSE, OR PHRASE?	NOUN, ADJ., OR ADV.?
1. <u>To sculpt this face</u> must have required a strong knowledge of the king's passions.	_____	_____
2. Perhaps the sculptor's hand mocked the king by etching those haughty passions permanently <u>into the face.</u>	_____	_____
3. <u>Clearly, the king's heart was fed by strong emotions.</u>	_____	_____
4. After all, how else could he have the confidence <u>to command his subjects?</u>	_____	_____
5. <u>Whatever the case was,</u> both men survive, in a way.	_____	_____
6. The sculptor survives in his handiwork, and the king survives in the sculpture <u>that represents him.</u>	_____	_____
7. Besides all that, <u>one irony stands out to me.</u>	_____	_____
8. Words on the pedestal command observers <u>to look around in awe at this king's works.</u>	_____	_____
9. <u>Looking around,</u> you see absolutely nothing.	_____	_____
10. Nothing, that is, except miles and miles <u>of flat, lonely sand.</u>	_____	_____

Phrases and Clauses

It's time to take a break from traditional grammar exercises. The following activities ask you to explore how people use phrases and clauses in the real world, outside your classroom walls. Which activity sparks your interest? Choose an activity to complete; then, with your teacher's approval, share the results with your classmates. Have a good time!

Color Me Smart

Type up the lyrics to one of your favorite songs. (Choose a song that is suitable for discussion in class.) Then use colored pencils to mark up the lyrics. Underline main clauses in blue. Underline subordinate clauses in red, and label the use of each clause (noun, adjective, or adverb). Then underline and label the use of each phrase. If you are really detail oriented, use a different color for each phrase type.

Bilingual Phrases

Explore how phrases are used in a language other than English. To do so, prepare two charts: one in English and one in another language. In the English chart, list types of phrases, their definitions, and two examples of each type used in a sentence. Then translate the entire chart into the other language. What changes do you observe? For example, the infinitive in English is *to* plus a verb, as in *to write.* But the infinitive in Spanish is a verb form ending in a vowel plus *r,* as in *escribir.* Use both charts to help yourself understand the concepts better.

See Jane run! See Jane laugh!

In a library, collect five or six books written for early readers, say, first and second graders. Analyze the texts' uses of clauses and phrases. For example, do sentences typically consist of main clauses *and* subordinate clauses, or just main clauses? Why do you think this is? What about the use of phrases? Are there lots of phrases, or just a few? Are there all *kinds* of phrases? Write a summary of your analysis, including your conclusions about why sentences are constructed this way for this age group.

Memorandum

Gather at least three business memos written by different people. Analyze the documents' uses of clauses and phrases, focusing on the quality of the sentences. Are sentences all the same length and structure, or is there variety? Does a writer use lots of main clauses but few subordinate clauses? Does a writer erroneously punctuate subordinate clauses as sentences? Do different types of phrases add variety to the sentences? Do you think one or more of the writers needs to change his or her use of clauses and phrases?

All the Difference

Take a well-known poem such as Robert Frost's "The Road Not Taken." Make sure the poem has lots of phrases in it. Rewrite the poem, replacing each phrase with an original phrase of your own. For example, *Two roads diverged in a yellow wood* could become *Two roads diverged at the edge of a city.* Use your phrases to create your own theme for the poem. For example, Frost's poem expresses quiet beauty and the satisfaction of a choice made well. You might express fast-paced action, danger, whimsy, regret, or fantasy. It's up to you—the phrases make all the difference!

Step by Step

A good set of instructions requires the careful use of clauses and phrases. Demonstrate your skill by writing step-by-step instructions for a process or procedure of your choosing. A few ideas are assembling a bicycle, installing software, and changing a tire. Then have a classmate follow your instructions to see how well you explained the process or procedure.

Phrases and Clauses

Directions: For each item, read the sentence. Then choose the best place in the sentence to insert the italicized word group. Circle the letter of your choice and write it on the blank.

Sample:

_____ **a.** Imagine hearing a train accident happen.

near your house

   A. before *Imagine*

   B. after *hearing*

   (C.) after *happen*

_____ **1.** You are only fifteen years old, but you realize to go for help.

that you are the only one available

   A. after *You*

   B. after *realize*

   C. after *help*

_____ **2.** This very emergency happened.

to fifteen-year-old Kate Shelley

   D. after *This*

   E. after *emergency*

   F. after *happened*

_____ **3.** One night Kate, listening to a rainstorm rage outside.

had stayed up late

   A. after *outside*

   B. after *rainstorm*

   C. after *Kate*

_____ **4.** At nearly midnight, she heard Engine Number Eleven near her house.

climbing the slope to Honey Creek Bridge

   D. before *At*

   E. before *she*

   F. after *Eleven*

_____ 5. The engine's passage was routine, but Kate wondered during the terrible storm.

why it was running

    A. after _but_

    B. after _wondered_

    C. after _storm_

_____ 6. Then a shocking crash sounded.

and water hissed

    D. before _Then_

    E. after _crash_

    F. after _sounded_

_____ 7. The hot engine had fallen from the bridge into the cold waters below.

which had broken

    A. after _engine_

    B. after _bridge_

    C. after _below_

_____ 8. Immediately, Kate thought of the midnight express, which was a passenger train due.

to cross the same bridge soon

    D. before _Kate_

    E. before _which_

    F. after _due_

_____ 9. She dashed out into the storm.

to go for help

    A. after _storm_

    B. after _She_

    C. after _dashed_

_____ 10. To reach the nearest source, she had to cross the 700-foot-long Des Moines River Bridge.

of help

    D. before _To_

    E. after _source_

    F. after _Bridge_

_____ 11. Kate finally reached the Moingona Station.
crawling slowly across the bridge

    A. before *Kate*

    B. after *reached*

    C. after *Station*

_____ 12. Here, the crash of Engine Number Eleven.
she announced

    D. after *Here,*

    E. after *crash*

    F. after *of*

_____ 13. That the midnight express had already been halted.
she learned

    A. before *That*

    B. after *That*

    C. after *halted*

_____ 14. Immediately she led a rescue party to the crash site of Engine Number Eleven.
where they saved two crew members

    D. after *Immediately*

    E. after *party*

    F. after *Eleven*

_____ 15. These fateful events occurred on July 6, 1881.
during the night

    A. before *These*

    B. after *events*

    C. after *occurred*

PART II

Directions: Circle the letter of the best revision of each item and write it on the blank. If no change is best, select the letter for *NO CHANGE.*

_____ 16. Where is the bookshelf? The one I made in shop class.

    A. NO CHANGE

    B. Where is the bookshelf that I made in shop class?

    C. Where is the bookshelf? That one I made in shop class.

    D. Where is the bookshelf in shop class?

_____ **17.** The stunt pilot entertained the crowd below. Flying in tricky patterns.

      F. NO CHANGE

      G. The stunt pilot entertained the crowd below flying in tricky patterns.

      H. The stunt pilot entertained the crowd flying in tricky patterns below.

      J. Flying in tricky patterns, the stunt pilot entertained the crowd below.

_____ **18.** Wishing the bell had rung already, the class seemed endless.

      A. NO CHANGE

      B. Wishing the bell had rung already, the class seemed endless to Esther.

      C. The class seemed endless, wishing the bell had rung already.

      D. Wishing the bell had rung already, Esther thought the class seemed endless.

_____ **19.** Walking to the bus stop hungry because I was in a hurry and skipped breakfast.

      F. NO CHANGE

      G. I was in a hurry and skipped breakfast because I walked to the bus stop.

      H. I walked to the bus stop hungry because I was in a hurry and skipped breakfast.

      J. I walked to the bus stop hungry. Because I was in a hurry and skipped breakfast.

_____ **20.** To get into a good college is the top priority of every teenager whom I know.

      A. NO CHANGE

      B. The top priority of every teenager whom I know to get into a good college.

      C. To get into a good college, whom I know, is the top priority of every teenager.

      D. To get into a good college. That is the top priority of every teenager whom I know.

The Four Sentence Types

There are four basic kinds of sentences: *simple, compound, complex,* and *compound-complex.* Each type is built from one or more clauses. As you know from your study of Part Three of this book, a *main clause* contains a subject and its verb and can stand alone as a sentence. A *subordinate clause* contains a subject and its verb but cannot stand alone as a sentence.

You will draw upon your knowledge of clauses to construct the four sentence types.

- The **simple sentence** has one main clause.
- The **compound sentence** has two or more main clauses.
- The **complex sentence** has one main clause and at least one subordinate clause.
- The **compound-complex sentence** has at least two main clauses and at least one subordinate clause.

In the following lessons, you will learn more about each of these sentence types, and you'll practice writing each type. In addition, you'll practice combining sentences to create a variety of sentence types in your writing.

17 The Simple Sentence

Every complete sentence has a **subject** and a **verb**. In the following sentences, the subject has one line under it; the verb has two.

Rain <u>fell</u>.

A <u>group</u> of students <u>gathered</u> for a study session.

These are *simple sentences*.

 A *simple sentence* contains one subject and one verb.

In other words, a simple sentence is made up of one main clause and no subordinate clauses.

SIMPLE SENTENCES: Reshma <u>wrote</u> an essay about the American Revolution.

The American Revolution <u>began</u> in 1775.

By 1883, the American colonies <u>had won</u> their independence.

In a simple sentence, either the subject or the verb, or both, may be *compound*. Something that is compound has two or more parts.

COMPOUND SUBJECT: Rain and hail <u>fell</u> heavily.

COMPOUND VERB: Rain <u>fell</u> heavily and <u>flooded</u> the roads.

COMPOUND SUBJECT AND VERB: Rain and hail <u>fell</u> heavily and <u>covered</u> the roads.

A compound subject counts as one subject, and a compound verb counts as one verb. In the examples above, each sentence is simple because it contains one subject and one verb.

ACTIVITY 1 ⎯⎯⎯⎯⎯⎯⎯⎯⎯⎯⎯⎯⎯⎯⎯⎯

Each numbered item consists of two sentences. Combine each pair into one simple sentence with either a compound subject or a compound verb. (Be sure to make necessary changes in capitalization, punctuation, and subject-verb agreement.)

Samples:

a. The skin of the mandarin fish smells bad. The skin also tastes bad.

The skin of the mandarin fish smells and tastes bad.

b. Hurricanes are a type of tropical storm. Typhoons are a type of tropical storm.

Hurricanes and typhoons are types of tropical storms.

1. Seals are prey to killer whales. Penguins are also prey to killer whales.

_____

_____

2. Tropical storms can sink ships. Tropical storms can wreck coastlines.

_____

_____

3. Hungry slugs can cause crop damage. Locusts can also cause crop damage.

_____

_____

4. European knights fought on horseback. They had many weapons.

_____

_____

5. The lance was a type of medieval weapon. The mace was another type.

_____

_____

6. The rainbow appears in daylight. It has seven arcs of color.

_____

_____

7. Some powerboats can go over 60 miles per hour. Some jet skis can go over 60 miles per hour.

_____

_____

8. Benjamin Franklin tied a key to a kite string. He flew the kite in a storm.

_____

_____

9. Benjamin Franklin was an American inventor. Thomas Edison was another American inventor.

_____

_____

10. The north pole of a magnet repels another north pole. It attracts a south pole.

_____

_____

Underline each simple sentence in the following passage. In this excerpt from George Bernard Shaw's play *Mrs. Warren's Profession,* Mrs. Warren and her daughter, Vivie, are arguing about differences in their ways of life. The simple sentences in Vivie's first set of lines are already underlined as samples.

from Mrs. Warren's Profession
George Bernard Shaw

VIVIE: Don't think for a moment I set myself above you in any way. <u>You attacked me with the conventional authority of a mother: I defended myself with the conventional superiority of a respectable woman.</u> Frankly, I am not going to stand any of your nonsense; and when you drop it I shall not expect you to stand any of mine. <u>I shall always respect your right to your own opinions and your own way of life.</u>

MRS. WARREN: My own opinions and my own way of life! Listen to [you] talking! Do you think I was brought up like you? able to pick and choose my own way of life? Do you think I did what I did because I liked it, or thought it right, or wouldn't rather have gone to college and been a lady if I'd had the chance?

VIVIE: Everybody has some choice, mother. The poorest girl alive may not be able to choose between being Queen of England or Principal of Newnham; but she can choose between ragpicking and flower-selling, according to her taste. People are always blaming their circumstances for what they are. I don't believe in circumstances. The people who get on in this world are the people who get up and look for the circumstances they want, and, if they can't find them, make them.

Writing
Application

Simple Sentences

In the excerpt from *Mrs. Warren's Profession,* the two women argue about the concept of fate. Mrs. Warren believes that her circumstances (in other words, fate) pushed her toward a certain way of life, while Vivie does not believe in circumstances. Instead, she believes that you make your own path. After reading the argument between Mrs. Warren and Vivie, with whom do you agree more?

On a separate sheet of paper, write **two** paragraphs of at least five sentences each. In them, explain whether you agree with Mrs. Warren or Vivie, and why. Give examples from real life to help explain your perspective. Finally, underline each simple sentence in your paragraphs.

LESSON 18 The Compound Sentence

Two or more simple sentences can be combined to form one *compound sentence.*

SIMPLE SENTENCE:	Taylor <u>plays</u> bass.
SIMPLE SENTENCE:	Brent <u>plays</u> the drums.
COMPOUND SENTENCE:	Taylor <u>plays</u> bass, and Brent <u>plays</u> the drums.

 A *compound sentence* contains two or more main clauses and no subordinate clauses.

In the compound sentences below, each main clause (simple sentence) is underlined.

COMPOUND SENTENCES: <u>My favorite actor is Jamie Foxx,</u> but <u>Norma's favorite is Brad Pitt.</u>

<u>In 2004 Foxx costarred with Tom Cruise in *Collateral,*</u> and <u>he played the lead role in *Ray.*</u>

<u>*Ray* is about the life of Ray Charles;</u> <u>Foxx is convincing as the singer/musician.</u>

In the examples above, notice that main clauses can be joined by a comma and a connecting word or by a semicolon.

ACTIVITY 1 _____

Decide whether each sentence is simple or compound. On the blank, write *S* for *simple sentence* or *C* for *compound sentence.*

> **Samples:**
>
> ___S___ **a.** Stealing ships and treasure, pirates have hunted the seas since ancient times.
>
> ___C___ **b.** *Buccaneer* is one word for a pirate, and *corsair* is another.

_____ **1.** In 78 B.C., Julius Caesar was captured and held for ransom by pirates.

_____ **2.** After six weeks, the twenty talents of gold was paid, and the pirates released Caesar.

_____ **3.** Intent on revenge, Caesar returned to the pirates' lair with a group of soldiers and killed them all.

_____ **4.** At this point, Caesar was just a young man, yet later, he would become the emperor of Rome.

_____ **5.** Charlotte de Berry was a fierce pirate in the mid-1600s, and Anne Bonny terrorized Spanish ships with Captain Jack Rackham in the early 1700s.

_____ **6.** On the Barbary Coast of Africa, the brothers Aruj and Khair ed-Din stalked European ships, and they were known as the Brothers Barbarossa.

_____ **7.** On the Indian Ocean, ships full of spices, ivory, and jewels were popular targets of pirates, and many were attacked.

_____ **8.** Henry Morgan and Blackbeard were inventive, colorful, and dangerous.

_____ **9.** In the 1920s, China was plagued by pirates, and Lai Choi San was one of these outlaws.

_____ **10.** She held wealthy people for ransom and stole valuable cargo and other items.

The clauses in a compound sentence are often joined by *coordinating conjunctions.* These conjunctions include *and, but, or, nor, for,* and *yet.*

I do not speak Swahili, *nor* do I speak Farsi.

I speak Spanish adequately, *and* I speak French well, *but* I speak English fluently.

QUESTION: Does a compound sentence need any special punctuation?

ANSWER: Yes, a comma usually precedes the conjunction in a compound sentence.

Michelle served the volleyball, *but* it hit the net.

QUESTION: Does it matter which conjunction I use to join simple sentences?

ANSWER: Yes, it matters. Different conjunctions have different purposes, as explained below.

1. Use *and* to join sentences that express equal thoughts.

   Mandy worked the crossword puzzle, *and* Julian read the comics.

2. Use *but* or *yet* to join sentences that contrast with each other.

   Mandy enjoys brain teasers, *but* Julian does not.

   The puzzle was difficult, *yet* Mandy easily finished it.

3. Use *or* or *nor* to join sentences that express two or more possibilities.

   Did Julian build this model ship, *or* did Jim build it?

   Jim is not interested in ships, *nor* did he build this model.

4. Use *for* to join sentences that express a cause and effect.

   Julian worked carefully, *for* he wanted the model to be perfect.

ACTIVITY 2 _____

Combine each pair of simple sentences to form a compound sentence. Use *and, but, or, nor, for,* or *yet.* Make changes directly to the printed sentences, as shown in the samples, or write your compound sentences on a separate sheet of paper (use the method your teacher prefers).

> **Samples:**
>   , but it
> **a.** Gym class can sometimes be boring, ~~It~~ can often be fun.
>   , nor am I
> **b.** I'm not good at basketball, ~~I'm not~~ good at softball.

1. Coach Webb blew his whistle. Everyone gathered around him.

2. He suggested playing dodgeball. No one wanted to play that game.

3. We could play softball. We could play volleyball.

4. We all like volleyball. Only twelve people can play at a time.

5. Finally, everyone agreed to play softball. Most of us could play all at once.

6. Carmen chose Seth for her team. She knew he was a good player.

7. Unfortunately, I couldn't bat well. I couldn't catch.

8. I was the last person to be chosen. I wasn't surprised.

9. Despite the slow beginning, the game was lively. Everyone had fun.

10. Carmen's team played well. In the end, my team was the winner.

ACTIVITY 3

Underline each compound sentence in the following passage. The first compound sentence is underlined as a sample.

The Civil Rights Act of 1964 was groundbreaking legislation. <u>It attacked racial discrimination head-on, but then so did the Civil Rights Act of 1866.</u> In 1866, the U.S. Civil War had recently ended, and freed slaves had a pressing need: citizenship. A hundred years later, the issue was not citizenship; it was problems of segregation and other discriminatory practices.

In 1866, despite freedom from slavery, blacks were barred from U.S. citizenship. They could not enter into legal contracts, own property, demand legal recourse, or claim other civil rights. The Civil Rights Act of 1866 remedied this discrimination, for it granted citizenship—and its rights—to all Americans, regardless of race or color. Likewise, the Civil Rights Act of 1964 protected against racial discrimination. Instead of granting citizenship, it banned discrimination by trade unions and specific types of employers; it guaranteed equal voting rights; and it prohibited segregation in public schools.

Both civil rights acts were extremely controversial and were difficult to put into law. In 1866, President Andrew Johnson vetoed the civil rights bill put before him, but legislators pushed the law through anyway. In 1963, President John F. Kennedy was unable to get a civil rights bill passed. But the next year, President Lyndon B. Johnson secured passage

of the Civil Rights Act of 1964. A century had passed since the first civil rights act, and now

the 1964 act gave federal law enforcement agencies the power to enforce equality in the

rights guaranteed by that first act.

Writing
Application

Compound Sentences

The rights of individuals has long been a hot topic in the United States. Whether the issue is children's rights, women's rights, workers' rights, or the right to equality for all races, people have many opinions. Their opinions often conflict.

Which category of rights strikes a chord with you? It may be an issue raised in the passage in Activity 3, or it may be one of those listed above in this box. Perhaps it is another category entirely.

On a separate sheet of paper, write two paragraphs of at least five sentences each, explaining your opinions about a certain type of rights. Explain who is entitled to the rights and why. Give examples from real life to support your explanation. In your paragraphs, use at least **five** compound sentences and underline each one. Check that you used commas and conjunctions, or semicolons, to join simple sentences.

19 The Complex Sentence

Although you may not realize it, you are already familiar with complex sentences. Think back to your study of main and subordinate clauses in Lesson 14. A complex sentence is simply a main clause joined to one or more subordinate clauses.

MAIN CLAUSE: we will rent a rowboat

SUBORDINATE CLAUSE: when the weather is nice

COMPLEX SENTENCE: When the weather is nice, we will rent a rowboat.

 A *complex sentence* has one main clause and at least one subordinate clause.

In the examples below, each main clause is underlined once, and each subordinate clause is underlined twice.

COMPLEX SENTENCES: This rowboat is unsafe because it has a leak in it.

If you try to use this boat, you will surely sink.

Please use a boat that passed inspection, which includes a check for seaworthiness.

Subordinate clauses are introduced by a word that makes the clause subordinate to, or dependent on, a main clause. You may want to review the three kinds of subordinate clauses covered in Lesson 14: noun clauses, adjective clauses, and adverb clauses. Here are some of the words that introduce subordinate clauses.

Words That Introduce Subordinate Clauses

Noun clauses often begin with . . .	how, that, what, whatever, when, where, whether, which, whichever, who, whoever, whom, whomever, whose, why
Adjective clauses begin with relative pronouns, which are . . .	who, whom, whose, which, that
Adverb clauses begin with subordinating conjunctions, which are . . .	after, although, as, because, before, if, since, so that, than, unless, until, when, where, whether, while

ACTIVITY 1

For each item below, you are given either a main clause or a subordinate clause. Use the clause to write a complex sentence.

> **Samples:**
>
> **a.** Marcos was late to history class.
>
>   Because he overslept, Marcos was late to history class.
>
> **b.** Unless we win this point.
>
>   We will lose the game unless we win this point.

1. The young man introduced himself to me.

_____

_____

2. How that happened.

_____

_____

3. Before you shut down the computer.

_____

_____

4. I'll meet you at my house.

_____

_____

5. Carina waited in the food court for an hour.

_____

_____

6. Whoever buys a ticket to opening night.

_____

_____

7. Whose ballet shoes these are.

_____

_____

8. When the dam crumbled.

_____

_____

9. Did you see the goal?

_____

_____

10. Please save a seat for me.

_____

_____

Combine each pair of sentences to make one complex sentence. If you need help, look again at the words that introduce subordinate clauses, located before Activity 1 in this lesson.

> **Sample:**
>
> Freddie wasn't sure. Magda was laughing.
>
> _Freddie wasn't sure why Magda was laughing._

1. Rebecca liked the blue sweater. She didn't buy it.

   _____

   _____

2. Bootsie escaped the yard. Someone left the gate ajar.

   _____

   _____

3. You must have a boarding pass. You can go through the security checkpoint.

   _____

   _____

4. You called me yesterday. I had already left for work.

   _____

   _____

5. Have you met Monique? Monique is new to school.

   _____

   _____

ACTIVITY 3 _____

Decide whether each sentence is simple, compound, or complex. On the blank, write S for _simple_, CD for _compound_, or CX for _complex_.

> **Samples:**
>
> _CD_ **a.** A common nickname for the football is "pigskin," and this name causes speculation.
>
> _S_ **b.** Are footballs really made of pigskin?
>
> _CX_ **c.** If they are not, what _are_ they made of?

_____ 1. Regulation NFL footballs are made of cowhide.

_____ 2. Wilson, which is the company that made the official footballs for the 2003 Super Bowl, uses the hides of steers.

_____ 3. To be used for this purpose, each steer must weigh around 1,000 pounds; the hide of one animal provides enough leather for 15 to 25 footballs.

_____ 4. For the 2003 Super Bowl, Wilson crafted 72 official balls at the Ada, Ohio, factory.

_____ 5. Each ball was marked with the Super Bowl logo, the date and location of the game, and the names of the two teams.

_____ 6. That year the teams were the Oakland Raiders and the Tampa Bay Buccaneers.

_____ 7. In part, these markings are a security precaution, for they help to prevent illegal substitution of "doctored" balls.

_____ 8. All NFL teams use footballs that are made of high-quality leather.

_____ 9. College teams do too, although NCAA footballs are slightly smaller than NFL footballs.

_____ 10. Not all footballs are made of cowhide, for cheaper models are made of synthetic materials such as vinyl.

_____ 11. Smaller footballs, which are designed for kids under age eight, may be made of easy-grip rubber.

_____ 12. Long ago, the football's inner bladder, which is the part that holds the air, was made from a pig's stomach.

_____ 13. Some people claim that the outsides of early footballs were made of pigskin.

_____ 14. They argue that this is how the ball got its nickname.

_____ 15. Others claim that the use of pigskin is only a myth.

 Writing
Application

Complex Sentences

Which is more important to you, sports or academics (your studies)? On a separate sheet of paper, write a paragraph of at least seven sentences answering this question. Use reasons and examples to support your point of view. In your paragraph, use at least **three** complex sentences.

With your teacher's approval, exchange papers with a classmate. Underline each complex sentence in the paragraph you are given. If you are not sure whether a sentence is complex, discuss it with your classmate or your teacher. Finally, share the results with your classmate.

20 The Compound-Complex Sentence

The *compound-complex sentence* is actually a combination of two other sentence types: the compound and the complex. Recall these types:

- The *compound sentence* has two or more main clauses and no subordinate clauses.

Esteban handed out notepads, and Kyra checked the sound system.
      MAIN CLAUSE   MAIN CLAUSE

- The *complex sentence* has one main clause and at least one subordinate clause.

As people arrived, Esteban handed out notepads.
   SUB. CLAUSE   MAIN CLAUSE

We can use the clauses in the examples above to form a compound-complex sentence.

As people arrived, Esteban handed out notepads, and Kyra checked the sound system.

 The *compound-complex sentence* has at least two main clauses and at least one subordinate clause.

Here are additional examples of compound-complex sentences. In the examples, each main clause is underlined once, and each subordinate clause is underlined twice.

Rowan cannot afford the boots unless she gets a job, but her mom won't buy them for her.

When Rahim heard the call for volunteers, he contacted the soup kitchen, and they gladly accepted his help.

Dougal has never been to Egypt, but he plans to go after he graduates from college.

ACTIVITY 1

Combine each group of sentences to form one compound-complex sentence. Use words from the list below, if needed, to introduce the subordinate clauses. (You can use any word more than once.) Write on the lines provided and underline each subordinate clause.

Hint: Be sure to use a comma and a coordinating conjunction (and, but, or) to join complete sentences.

after	although	because	before	if	since
so that	that	until	when	which	while

a. Insecticides kill insects. Insects damage crops. Insecticides can also kill harmless creatures.

Insecticides kill insects that damage crops, but they can also kill harmless creatures.

(Notice that a comma and __but__ join the complex sentence to the simple sentence in the revision. The subordinate clause is that damage crops.)

b. I wondered. Who had set off the fire alarm? I soon found out.

I wondered who had set off the fire alarm, and I soon found out.

(Notice that a comma and __and__ join the complex sentence to the simple sentence in the revision. The subordinate clause is who had set off the fire alarm.)

1. I often get up. The sun rises. I go jogging with my friend Kayla.

_____

_____

2. The telephone rang. Kathy ran to answer it. The caller had already hung up.

_____

_____

3. We can eat now. We could eat later. We're sure to be on time for the show.

_____

_____

4. The deer raced away. It smelled the hunter. It sensed danger.

_____

_____

5. I wondered. What had happened? No one would tell me.

_____

_____

6. I sat on the patio. It got dark and chilly. Then I went inside.

_____

_____

7. Cal left Alaska. It is our nation's biggest state. He settled happily in tiny Maine.

_____

_____

8. The cliff was steep. The climbers reached the top. They used specialized equipment.

_____

_____

9. Many people check their e-mail. They are aghast. The Inbox is full of spam.

_____

_____

10. You will rent a movie. I'll make some snacks. We can have a fun evening together.

_____

_____

ACTIVITY 2 _____

Identify each sentence's type by writing one of these abbreviations on the blank:

S for *simple*   CX for *complex*

CD for *compound*   Cd-Cx for *compound-complex*

Samples:

_Cd-Cx_ **a.** Many people have heard the phrase "the real McCoy," but they don't know how it originated.

__S__ **b.** In fact, the phrase sprang up in response to an inventor.

__CD__ **c.** The inventor's name was Elijah McCoy, and he lived from 1844 to 1929.

__Cx__ **d.** Elijah was one of those teenagers whom people describe as being good with machines.

_____ **1.** For Elijah, tools and machines were not just a hobby; they were a passion.

_____ **2.** As an adult, McCoy patented more than fifty inventions that included tire tread, shoe heels, an ironing table, and many others.

_____ **3.** By far, his most memorable invention was the automatic oil cup, which was used on locomotives to drip oil automatically on moving parts.

_____ **4.** McCoy's invention was so popular that other inventors tried to imitate it, but people preferred "the real McCoy."

_____ **5.** They asked for it specifically.

_____ **6.** McCoy was born to former slaves who had escaped from Kentucky to Canada on the Underground Railroad.

_____ **7.** George and Emillia settled in Colchester, Ontario, and Elijah was born on May 2, 1844.

_____ **8.** By the time he was a teenager, he already showed great promise in working with machines, and at age sixteen, he went to Scotland to study.

_____ **9.** He pursued his favorite subject matter, mechanical engineering, which concerns the design and production of tools and machines.

_____ **10.** Afterward, McCoy settled in Michigan.

_____ **11.** By this time, Abraham Lincoln had issued the Emancipation Proclamation, and slavery was outlawed in the United States.

_____ **12.** For many years McCoy worked as a fireman and oilman on the Michigan Central Railroad, where his work inspired many of his inventions; one of these was the famous oil cup.

_____ **13.** In 1882 he left the railroad to spend more time on his inventions.

_____ **14.** He worked so hard that sometimes he patented two or three devices a year.

_____ **15.** He died in 1929.

ACTIVITY 3 _____

Read the passage and answer the questions that follow. The sentences have been numbered. The events in the passage occur around 1884 in Wabash, Indiana. The speaker, a Sioux Indian girl, has been sent to a Quaker boarding school for education. She has just learned that school officials intend to cut her hair short. In her Sioux culture, short hair is the mark of a coward.

from **The School Days of an Indian Girl**
Gertrude Simmons Bonnin (Zitkala-Ṡa)

(1) I watched my chance, and when no one noticed I disappeared. **(2)** I crept up the stairs as quietly as I could in my squeaking shoes[;] my moccasins had been exchanged for shoes. **(3)** Along the hall I passed, without knowing whither I was going. **(4)** Turning aside to an open door, I found a large room with three white beds in it. . . . **(5)** On my hands and knees I crawled under [a] bed, and cuddled myself in the dark corner.

(6) From my hiding place I peered out, shuddering with fear whenever I heard footsteps near by. **(7)** Though in the hall loud voices were calling my name, and I knew that even Judéwin was searching for me, I did not open my mouth to answer. **(8)** Then the steps were quickened and the voices became excited. **(9)** The sounds came nearer and nearer. **(10)** Women and girls entered the room. **(11)** I held my breath, and watched them open closet doors and peep behind large trunks. . . . **(12)** What caused them to stoop and look under the bed I do not know. **(13)** I remember being dragged out, though I resisted by kicking and scratching wildly. **(14)** In spite of myself, I was carried downstairs and tied fast in a chair.

(15) I cried aloud, shaking my head all the while until I felt the cold blades of the scissors against my neck, and heard them gnaw off one of my thick braids. **(16)** Then I lost my spirit. . . . **(17)** In my anguish I moaned for my mother, but no one came to comfort me. **(18)** Not a soul reasoned quietly with me, as my own mother used to do; for now I was only one of many little animals driven by a herder.

1. Which sentences in the passage are compound-complex? Write the number of each compound-complex sentence on the following blanks.

   _____   _____   _____   _____

2. Out of the eighteen sentences in this excerpt, only four are compound-complex. Why do you think there are not more compound-complex sentences?

   _____

   _____

   _____

3. Sentence 6 is not compound-complex, but with a quick revision, it could be. On the lines below, rewrite sentence 6 as a compound-complex sentence.

   _____

   _____

   _____

4. Sentence 15 is not compound-complex, but with the addition of one word—*I*—it would be. On the lines below, rewrite sentence 15 as a compound-complex sentence.

   _____

   _____

   _____

5. Do you think the school officials were within their rights to cut the speaker's hair? Why or why not? On the lines below, write at least **five** sentences explaining your opinion. Use at least **one** compound-complex sentence and underline it.

   _____

   _____

   _____

   _____

   _____

   _____

   _____

   _____

LESSON

21 Review of Sentence Types

- A *simple sentence* contains one subject and one verb (one main clause).
- A *compound sentence* contains two or more main clauses and no subordinate clauses.
- A *complex sentence* has one main clause and at least one subordinate clause.
- A *compound-complex sentence* has at least two main clauses and at least one subordinate clause.

ACTIVITY 1 _____

Each sentence in the following passage is numbered. On the blank that corresponds with each number, identify the sentence's type by writing one of these abbreviations:

S for *simple*   CX for *complex*

CD for *compound*   Cd-Cx for *compound-complex*

Sample paragraph:

ᵃThe term "comedy," as it used to describe a literary category, does not necessarily mean "hilarious." ᵇComedies contrast to other categories in one main way. ᶜThey end happily, and they often feature a marriage. ᵈIn contrast, the tragedies end in tragedy, and the histories follow the course of a real life, while romances feature altered reality.

a. __CX__

b. __S__

c. __CD__

d. __Cd-Cx__

---

¹For many young people, days roar along like an emotional roller coaster. ²One moment life is a bowl of cherries—with none of the pits—and the next moment, life is hearts and flowers and little Cupids. ³Then, with no warning, life takes a nosedive that reaches the depths of despair. ⁴What's a person to do during all this turmoil? ⁵Read Shakespeare!

⁶No matter what your mood is, there is a Shakespearean play for you; you just have to find it. ⁷The great bard's dramas group into four categories: comedies, romances, tragedies, and

1. _____

2. _____

3. _____

4. _____

5. _____

6. _____

7. _____

8. _____

9. _____

histories. [8]If you are feeling lighthearted, happy, or in the mood for fun, then reach for a comedy. [9]In this category are thirteen plays, including *As You Like It, Much Ado About Nothing,* and *A Midsummer Night's Dream.* [10]Pranksters, clowns,* and sweethearts will entertain you.

[11]If you need an escape from reality, reach for the romances, for you'll find flights of fancy and remote, enchanted settings. [12]Most remarkable is *The Tempest,* which is the tale of Prospero and his daughter, Miranda, who are shipwrecked on an enchanted island.

[13]Misery loves company, so when you're feeling miserable, lose yourself in a Shakespearean tragedy. [14]In this category are some of the bard's most famous works, which include *Romeo and Juliet, Macbeth, Julius Caesar, King Lear,* and others. [15]The gamut of tragedy—from star-crossed lovers to murder to betrayal to insanity—is played out on the pages of these plays.

[16]Finally, in serious or studious moods, read one of the histories. [17]Mainly they tell the stories of kings of England: Henry VI, Richard III, Henry the VIII, and others. [18]These plays take you deep into the characters of the rulers, but don't fret. [19]If the history starts to put you to sleep, just set it aside and reach for a comedy! [20]Or grab a tragedy . . . or a romance. . . .

clown: a country fellow; joker; buffoon

10. _____

11. _____

12. _____

13. _____

14. _____

15. _____

16. _____

17. _____

18. _____

19. _____

20. _____

ACTIVITY 2

Answer each question with a simple sentence. Write your sentence on the line provided.

> **Sample:**
>
> Which category of Shakespearean play reflects your mood today?
>
> _The comedy category reflects my mood today._

1. Which category of Shakespearean play do you think you'd enjoy reading most?

   _____

2. What is one Shakespearean play you have read or seen performed?

   _____

3. If you could star in any Shakespearean play, which one would it be?

   _____

4. Who would you cast as your costar?

   _____

5. If you could ask Shakespeare one question, what would it be?

   _____

ACTIVITY 3

Revise each sentence you wrote in Activity 2 to be a complex sentence. To do so, add a subordinate clause to the main clause that you wrote. Write your new sentences on the lines provided.

> **Sample:**
>
> _(The following sample is a revision of the sample in Activity 2.)_
>
> _The comedy category reflects my mood today because I feel upbeat and cheerful._

1. _____

   _____

2. _____

   _____

3. _____

   _____

4. _____

_____

5. _____

_____

ACTIVITY 4 _____

Use coordinating conjunctions to combine each pair of simple sentences into one compound sentence. Make your changes directly to the printed sentences, as shown in the samples.

> **Samples:**
>
>   , and my
> **a.** Some of the best CDs are movie soundtracks. ~~My~~ favorite is *The Blues Brothers.*
>
>   , but
> **b.** I did not see this movie in a theater. I saw it on a rental DVD.

1. On this CD, Aretha Franklin sings "Think." John Belushi and Dan Aykroyd sing "Everybody Needs Somebody to Love."

2. Listening to a movie soundtrack sparks my imagination. I remember scenes from the film vividly.

3. Sci-fi fans may like the *Star Wars* soundtrack. They may prefer the tracks from *Spider-Man 2.*

4. My sister's favorite soundtrack is *Lost in Translation.* I haven't heard this one.

5. Fans of "oldie" movies will love the *Gone With the Wind* soundtrack. They'll also like the *Lawrence of Arabia* tracks.

ACTIVITY 5 _____

Combine the clauses in each group below into one compound-complex sentence. Choose appropriate words to introduce the subordinate clauses. Make your changes directly to the printed sentences, as shown in the samples.

> **Samples:**
>
>   , but they   when people
> **a.** Cell phones are convenient. ~~They~~ can also be disruptive. ~~People~~ use them in public places.
>
>   , or they
> **b.** Cell phones are banned from some classrooms. ~~They~~ are banned from school
>   if there
> buildings entirely. ~~There~~ is a problem with usage.

1. During a movie is no time to take a call. People do it anyway. They can't stand to turn off the phone.

2. Other people flip open the lighted display on their phones. They check for text messages. The movie has started.

3. People are sitting behind them. They are flashed by the light of the display panel. It interrupts their enjoyment of the movie.

4. They are standing in a checkout line. Shoppers make a call and talk to their friend. The cashier must interrupt to ask about payment.

5. In line behind the shopper stand other people. They hear the entire phone call. They are wishing the caller would just hang up, pay, and move along.

Sentence Types

It's time to take a break from traditional grammar exercises. The following activities ask you to explore how people use the four sentence types in the real world, outside your classroom walls. Which activity sparks your interest? Choose an activity to complete; then, with your teacher's approval, share the results with your classmates. Have a good time!

Teen-Friendly

What makes a book written for a teen audience truly teen-friendly? Gather at least five books published for the teen market and make a list of elements to evaluate. In the list, include sentence types; other elements could include characters, theme, plot, etc. How does each author handle these elements? For example, do simple and compound sentences dominate the text, or are complex and compound-complex sentences included too? Use your findings to explain what makes a book teen-friendly.

Tell Me

Do you know someone whose life—past or present—interests you? Arrange a time to interview this person. Record the interview, then transcribe it onto paper. Now analyze your interviewee's use of clauses in his or her speech. Does the person tend to speak in simple sentences, complex sentences, or other sentence types? What about your own speech? What conclusions can you draw about sentence types and spoken conversation?

Poetry Under Construction

Find a poem you like that is made up mostly of clauses rather than phrases. On a sheet of paper, write the poem in sentence style instead of in stanzas. Use the type of each clause—main or subordinate—to decide how to arrange and punctuate the sentences. Now, using this sentence version as inspiration, write your own set of sentences of a similar length. You may want to express your thoughts or feelings regarding the poem. Finally, arrange your sentences into stanzas to create an original poem.

Read All About It

Grab a section of the newspaper—sports, arts, whatever—and choose an article to study. Your task? Tabulate how many of each sentence type the article contains and use the data to form theories about newspapers. In terms of reading difficulty, what does the distribution of sentence types say about readers? About the writers? About the article's purpose? (For example, is the purpose to inform quickly, to engage readers with elaborate text, or something else?) Compare research with someone who read a different newspaper section.

In Other Words . . .

A translator faces the challenge of accurately representing ideas expressed by subordinate clauses. For example, *Talks between the dignitaries was productive even though they voiced opposing ideas* is different from *Talks between the dignitaries was productive because they voiced opposing ideas.* Test your bilingual skills by translating an article, speech, or other document from another language into English. Pay attention to sentence types in the original language and strive to construct the same types in English.

Readability Statistics

Some word-processing programs can tabulate a document's reading level. For example, an 11 indicates an eleventh-grade reading level. In Microsoft Word, click "show readability statistics" in the Spelling and Grammar section of Options, in the Tools menu. Run the spelling/grammar check; at the end, a box pops up showing the text's reading level. Run this feature on a paper you have written. Experiment to see how the reading level changes if you increase the number of complex and compound-complex sentences. What happens when you revise the sentences to be mostly simple and/or compound?

TEST PRACTICE
Sentence Types

PART I

Directions: On each blank, identify the sentence's type by writing the appropriate letter, as listed below:

A   *simple sentence*

B   *compound sentence*

C   *complex sentence*

D   *compound-complex sentence*

Samples:

___C___ **a.** There are more languages in our world than there are countries.

___D___ **b.** Many people know more than one language, or they know a little bit of a second language that they have studied.

_____ **1.** If aliens exist, what language do they speak?

_____ **2.** A space probe named *Voyager 1* is traveling out into deep space.

_____ **3.** On it is a gold-plated record that has words and sounds recorded on it.

_____ **4.** It contains greetings in sixty different languages, and it also contains various sounds from nature.

_____ **5.** The idea is that aliens could listen to the recording, and they would have an idea of what Earth is like.

_____ **6.** In Puerto Rico, the Arecibo dish picks up radio signals that come from deep in the galaxy.

_____ **7.** Using the incoming signals, scientists can map faraway planets and stars.

_____ **8.** Some people have wondered whether aliens might one day contact us through this dish.

_____ **9.** The signals that the dish picks up are many light-years old, for they took that long to reach Earth.

_____**10.** If aliens did send a signal to the dish, the signal would be light-years old when we got it.

Directions: Circle the letter of the best revision of each item and write it on the blank. If the item needs no change, select the letter for *NO CHANGE*.

_____ **11.** Samuel Clemens used a pen name. It was Mark Twain. He is the author of humorous short stories and novels.

    A. NO CHANGE

    B. Samuel Clemens used a pen name. Which was Mark Twain. He is the author of humorous short stories and novels.

    C. Samuel Clemens used a pen name, and Mark Twain is the author of humorous short stories and novels.

    D. Samuel Clemens, who used the pen name Mark Twain, is the author of humorous short stories and novels.

_____ **12.** One novel that is popular with children and adults alike is *The Adventures of Tom Sawyer.*

    F. NO CHANGE

    G. One novel is popular. Children and adults like it. It is *The Adventures of Tom Sawyer.*

    H. One novel that is popular with children and adults alike. It is *The Adventures of Tom Sawyer.*

    J. One novel that is popular with children and adults alike, and the name of the novel is *The Adventures of Tom Sawyer.*

_____ **13.** This tale includes characters, and they are Tom Sawyer, Huckleberry Finn, and Aunt Sally.

    A. NO CHANGE

    B. This tale's characters include Tom Sawyer, Huckleberry Finn, and Aunt Sally.

    C. This tale's characters include Tom Sawyer. They also include Huckleberry Finn and Aunt Sally.

    D. This tale's characters, which include Tom Sawyer, Huckleberry Finn, and Aunt Sally.

_____ **14.** One of the best-known scenes, in which Tom is given the chore of whitewashing (painting) a fence.

    F. NO CHANGE

    G. One of the best-known scenes. Tom is given the chore of whitewashing (painting) a fence.

    H. One of the best-known scenes is the one in which Tom is given the chore of whitewashing (painting) a fence.

    J. One of the best-known scenes is the chore of whitewashing (painting) a fence.

_____ **15.** What an awful chore for a summer day!

    A. NO CHANGE

    B. What an awful chore, which is for a summer day!

C. What an awful chore. For a summer day!

D. Which is an awful chore for a summer day!

_____ **16.** Of course he doesn't want to do the work. He devises a clever plan.

    F. NO CHANGE

    G. Of course he doesn't want to do the work, and he devises a clever plan.

    H. Of course he doesn't want to do the work, which devises a clever plan.

    J. Because he doesn't want to do the work. He devises a clever plan.

_____ **17.** He pretends to have a fantastic time painting the fence. Until another boy sees him. The other boy comes over.

    A. NO CHANGE

    B. He pretends to have a fantastic time painting the fence. Until another boy sees him and comes over.

    C. He pretends to have a fantastic time painting the fence until another boy sees him. The other boy comes over.

    D. He pretends to have a fantastic time painting the fence until another boy sees him and comes over.

_____ **18.** Since the "chore" looks like fun, this boy wants to paint too, and he asks for a brush.

    F. NO CHANGE

    G. Since the "chore" looks like fun. This boy wants to paint too, and he asks for a brush.

    H. Since the "chore" looks like fun, this boy wants to paint too. Asking for a brush.

    J. The "chore," which looks like fun. This boy wants to paint too, and he asks for a brush.

_____ **19.** Other boys come along. After a while. Tom is relaxing. Others do the work for him.

    A. NO CHANGE

    B. Other boys come along after a while. Tom is relaxing. While others do the work for him.

    C. Other boys come along; after a while, Tom is relaxing while others do the work for him.

    D. Other boys come along; after a while, Tom is relaxing. While others do the work for him.

_____ **20.** Twain is known for his humorous, enjoyable tales. Twain is known for his stories' portrayal of the South.

    F. NO CHANGE

    G. Twain is known for his humorous, enjoyable tales. Which portray the South.

    H. Twain is known for his humorous, enjoyable tales and for his stories' portrayal of the South.

    J. Twain, known for his humorous, enjoyable tales, his stories' portrayal of the South.

Grammar, Mechanics, Phrases, Clauses, and Sentences

PART I _____

Directions: In each item, certain words are underlined and labeled. Circle the letter of the underlined part that contains an error. If the item has no error, choose *E* for *No error.*

_____ 1. A *jester,* sometimes called a fool, <u>was</u> a person <u>who</u> provided entertainment to
        A   **B**   **C**
      a <u>kings</u> household. <u>No error</u>
          D   **E**

_____ 2. For <u>example,</u> a jester <u>might say or do</u> ridiculous things just <u>to making</u> people
              A   **B**   **C**
      smile <u>or</u> laugh. <u>No error</u>
            D   **E**

_____ 3. If you <u>thinks</u> about <u>it,</u> a jester <u>is</u> much like <u>a</u> modern-day class clown. <u>No error</u>
              A   **B**   **C**   **D**   **E**

_____ 4. <u>Frequently,</u> the <u>jester's</u> outfit <u>consisted</u> of multicolored <u>clothing,</u> a many-pointed
          A   **B**   **C**   **D**
      cap, and bells. <u>No error</u>
                     E

_____ 5. You may be <u>surprised</u> to learn <u>this:</u> Jesters <u>was</u> a part of the courts of <u>Egyptian</u>
                 A   **B**   **C**   **D**
      pharaohs. <u>No error</u>
               E

_____ 6. The <u>anceint</u> Aztecs of <u>Mexico</u> enjoyed jesters as <u>well, for</u> these comedians reg-
             A   **B**   **C**
      ularly provided comic relief to <u>their</u> patrons. <u>No error</u>
                              D   **E**

_____ 7. In <u>centuries</u> past, <u>England's</u> royal courts <u>enjoy</u> jesters' <u>jokes,</u> performances, and
           A   **B**   **C**   **D**
      madness—real or pretended. <u>No error</u>
                           E

_____ 8. Some jesters <u>were</u> truly <u>mad. While</u> others <u>merely</u> pretended that <u>they</u> were
                  A   **B**   **C**   **D**
      insane. <u>No error</u>
               E

_____ 9. <u>At</u> times, a jester might poke fun at the <u>king</u> by <u>imitating</u> his mannerisms <u>or</u>
      A   **B**   **C**   **D**
      speech habits. <u>No error</u>
                 E

_____ **10.** <u>Today's</u> jesters who <u>routine</u> poke fun at those who <u>are</u> in power <u>are</u> late-night talk
    A   B   C   D

show hosts. <u>No error</u>
    E

PART II

Directions: Look carefully at each item for one or more errors in grammar, mechanics, or sentence structure. Circle the letter of the best revision of each item and write it on the blank. If the item needs no change, select the letter for *NO CHANGE*.

_____ **11.** On the first Tuesday of each month, the committee meet to discuss new business and to follow through on old business.

    A. NO CHANGE

    B. On the first Tuesday of each month, the committee meets to discuss new business and to follow through on old business.

    C. On the first Tuesday of each month, and the committee meet to discuss new business and to follow through on old business.

    D. On the first Tuesday of each month, the committee meet. To discuss new business and to follow through on old business.

_____ **12.** Mrs. Brazos is proud of her daughter, for she has took singing lessons since she was seven years old and can sing like an angel.

    F. NO CHANGE

    G. Mrs. Brazos is proud of her daughter, for she has take singing lessons since she was seven years old and can sing like an angel.

    H. Mrs. Brazos is proud of her daughter, for she has taken singing lessons since she was seven years old and can sing like an angel.

    J. Mrs. Brazos is proud of her daughter, for she has taking singing lessons since she was seven years old and can sing like an angel.

_____ **13.** Although the train tracks are two blocks from Seth's apartment. He can still hear the train shrieking along the tracks.

    A. NO CHANGE

    B. Although the train tracks is two blocks from Seth's apartment. He can still hear the train shrieking along the tracks.

    C. Although the train tracks are two blocks from Seth's apartment, he can still hear the train shrieking along the tracks.

    D. Although the train tracks are two blocks from Seth's apartment; he can still hear the train shrieking along the tracks.

_____ **14.** I'll except your excuse this one time, but your not excused from taking the quiz you missed by being late.

    F. NO CHANGE

    G. I'll accept your excuse this one time, but your not excused from taking the quiz you missed by being late.

H. I'll except your excuse this one time, but you're not excused from taking the quiz you missed by being late.

J. I'll accept your excuse this one time, but you're not excused from taking the quiz you missed by being late.

_____ **15.** I'm real sorry you don't like the flower arrangment; perhaps I could replace the tulips with roses.

    A. NO CHANGE

    B. I'm really sorry you don't like the flower arrangement; perhaps I could replace the tulips with roses.

    C. I'm real sorry you dont' like the flower arrangement; perhaps I could replace the tulips with roses.

    D. I'm really sorry you don't like the flower arrangment perhaps I could replace the tulips with roses.

_____ **16.** Puffing out in the stiff breeze, Gavin worked to control the sails on the sailboat that he had rented.

    F. NO CHANGE

    G. Gavin worked to control the sails, puffing out in the stiff breeze, on the sailboat that he had rented.

    H. Puffing out in the stiff breeze on the sailboat, Gavin worked to control the sails that he had rented.

    J. Puffing out in the stiff breeze, Gavin worked to control the sails that he had rented on the sailboat.

_____ **17.** Every Saturday morning, Adam takes his basketball over to the neighborhood court and joins in a pickup game.

    A. NO CHANGE

    B. Every Saturday morning, Adam takes his basketball over to the neighborhood court. And joins in a pickup game.

    C. Every Saturday morning, which Adam takes his basketball over to the neighborhood court and joins in a pickup game.

    D. Every Saturday morning over to the neighborhood court, Adam takes his basketball and joins in a pickup game.

_____ **18.** Turned up to an extremely high volume, it was hard to concentrate on doing homework.

    F. NO CHANGE

    G. Turned up to an extremely high volume. It was hard to concentrate on doing homework.

    H. Turned up to an extremely high volume, the television made it hard to concentrate on doing homework.

    J. Turned up to an extremely high volume, Amanda realized it was hard to concentrate on doing homework.

_____ **19.** Two boys walked into a pizza parlor. One turns to the other and says, "I hope you're paying, because I'm penniless."

    A. NO CHANGE

    B. Two boys walked into a pizza parlor. One turns to the other and says, "I hope you're paying, because I'm pennyless."

    C. Two boys walked into a pizza parlor because one turns to the other and says, "I hope you're paying, because I'm penniless."

    D. Two boys walked into a pizza parlor. One turned to the other and said, "I hope you're paying, because I'm penniless."

_____ **20.** Each student can have their yearbook photo taken a second time if they don't like the first photo.

    F. NO CHANGE

    G. All students can have their yearbook photos taken a second time if they don't like the first photos.

    H. Each student can have their yearbook photo taken a second time, if they don't like the first photo.

    J. If they don't like the first photo, each student can have their yearbook photo taken a second time.

Glossary

adjective

A word that modifies a noun or a pronoun. Certain prepositional phrases, participial phrases, infinitive phrases, and subordinate clauses may be used as adjectives.

adverb

A word that modifies a verb, an adjective, or an adverb. Certain prepositional phrases, infinitive phrases, and subordinate clauses may be used as adverbs.

agreement

A subject and its verb are both expressed in the same number (singular or plural), or a pronoun and its antecedent are both expressed in the same number and gender (male, female, or neuter).

clause

A related sequence of words that has a subject and a predicate. A *main clause* can stand alone as a sentence, but a *subordinate clause* cannot stand alone as a complete sentence.

complex sentence

A sentence containing one main clause and at least one subordinate clause.

compound sentence

A sentence containing two or more main clauses and no subordinate clauses.

compound-complex sentence

A sentence containing at least two main clauses and at least one subordinate clause.

degrees of comparison

The degrees of comparison are the *positive degree*, used to modify one thing; the *comparative degree*, used to modify two things; and the *superlative degree*, used to modify more than two things.

double negative

The use of more than one "no" word in a sentence, as in *I don't know nothing*.

gerund

A verb form used as a noun in a sentence. A gerund ends in *ing*.

gerund phrase

A phrase made up of a gerund and any objects, modifiers, and/or complements. It is used as a noun.

infinitive

A verb form that can be used as a noun, an adjective, or an adverb. Most infinitives begin with *to*, as in *to forgive*.

infinitive phrase

A phrase made up of an infinitive and any objects, modifiers, or complements. The phrase is used as a noun, an adjective, or an adverb.

modifier

A word, phrase, or clause that describes a word or word group. Modifiers are either adjectives or adverbs.

participial phrase

A phrase made up of a participle and any objects, modifiers, and/or complements. It is used as an adjective.

participle

A verb form that may be used as part of a verb phrase or as an adjective.

phrase	A related sequence of words that does not have a subject and/or a predicate and that is used as a single part of speech.
predicate	The part of a sentence that says something about the subject.
prepositional phrase	A phrase made up of a preposition, its object, and any modifiers of that object.
simple sentence	A sentence containing one subject and one verb (one main clause).
subject	The word or word group about which the predicate says something.
tense	Used in reference to a verb, *tense* indicates the time of the action or of the state of being.
verb	Part of speech that expresses action or links the subject to another word in the sentence.
verbal	A verb form that is not used as a verb, but rather as a noun, an adjective, or an adverb.
verbal phrase	A phrase made up of a verbal and any objects, modifiers, and/or complements. See *gerund phrase, infinitive phrase,* and *participial phrase.*

Index

A

Abbreviations
    for addresses, 99
    for book parts, 99
    for titles, 99
    for years, 99
Abstract nouns, 39
accept, except, 34, 35, 97
according to, subject-verb agreement
    and, 32
Acronyms, 99
Action verbs, 2, 36
Addresses, abbreviations for, 99
Adjective(s), 2, 46, 71, 198
    articles as, 6, 43, 47, 49
    degrees of comparison, 49–50, 71,
        198
    distinguishing from adverbs, 54
    infinitives used as, 128
    nouns as, 14
    types of, 47
    verbals as, 122
Adjective clauses, 137, 138, 156
    relative pronouns to begin, 139,
        175
    setting off with commas, 140
Adjective phrases, 113–114, 153
Adverb(s), 2, 46, 71, 198
    degrees of comparison, 49–50, 71,
        198
    distinguishing from adjectives,
        54
    infinitives used as, 128
    verbals as, 122
Adverb clauses, 137, 141–143, 156
    punctuating, 143
    subordinate conjunctions in
        introducing, 141, 175
Adverb phrases, 115, 153
affect, effect, 34, 35
Agreement, 198
    pronoun-antecedent, 62, 71
    subject-verb, 30–33
Antecedent, 2, 63, 71
    pronoun agreement with, 62, 71
anyway, 57
anywhere, 57
Apostrophes, 94, 106
    to form contractions, 77
    to form possessives, 77
Appositives, 80
Articles *(a, an, the),* 6, 43, 47, 49
as well as, subject-verb agreement and,
    32

B

be, forms of, 31
besides/except, 120
bring, take, 35
by/until, 120–121

C

Capitalization
    of first and main words in titles, 84
    of first word and nouns in salutation,
        84
    of first word in a sentence, 84
    of first word in closing of a letter, 84
    of first word in direct quotation, 84
    of *I,* 84
    of names in direct address, 84
    of proper nouns and adjectives,
        2, 84
    of school subjects, 87
    of sections of the country, 84
    in travel writing, 88
    in writing about poetry, 86
Clauses, 111, 132, 156, 198
    adjective, 138, 156
    adverb, 137, 141–143, 156
    main or independent, 111, 132, 133,
        156, 167
    noun, 137, 138, 156
    subordinate or dependent, 111, 132,
        134, 137, 156, 167, 175
Closing of letter, capitalization of words
    in, 84
Collective nouns, 40–41
Colons, to call attention to what follows,
    77
Commas
    after prepositional phrases, 79
    in forming compound sentences, 77,
        171
    with quotation marks, 80
    in series, 77
    to set off adjective clauses, 140
    to set off appositives, 80
    to set off interrupting words and
        expressions, 77
    to set off introductory word, phrase
        or clause, 77
Comparative degree of comparison, 50,
    51, 198
Complex sentences, 178, 179, 184,
    198
Compound-complex sentences, 179,
    184, 198
Compound object, 2
Compound sentences, 171, 172, 174,
    179, 184, 198
Compound subject, 32, 33, 61, 168
Compound verb, 168
Concrete nouns, 39, 42
Conjunctions, 2
    coordinating, 2, 9, 172, 179, 187
    subordinate, 141, 175
Contractions, 56, 77, 83
Coordinating conjunctions, 2, 9, 172,
    179, 187
Count nouns, 42–45

D

Dangling modifiers, 148–149, 158
Degrees of comparison, 49–50, 71,
    198
Demonstratives, 47, 48
Dependent clauses. *See* Subordinate
    clauses
Dialogue, 83
    quotation marks in, 81
Dictionaries, using, for spelling, 98
Direct address, capitalization of names
    in, 84, 86
Double negatives, 56, 71, 105, 198

E

effect, affect, 34, 35
ESL Focus
    articles, 49
        with count and noncount nouns,
            43
        gerund and infinitive phrases after
            verbs, 130
        present progressive and the present
            tenses, 23
everywhere, 57
except, accept, 34, 35, 97
except/besides, 120
Exclamation points, with quotation
    marks, 81

F

Future perfect progressive tense, 23
Future perfect tense, 22–24
Future progressive tense, 23
Future tense, 22–24

G

Gerund(s), 123, 198
Gerund phrases, 123–124, 130, 153,
    198
Grammar, 21, 104

H

have, forms of, 22, 31
Helping verbs, 26

I

I, capitalization of, 84
including, subject-verb agreement and,
    32
Indefinite pronouns, 65–66
Independent clauses. *See* Main clauses
Infinitive, 128, 198
Infinitive phrases, 128–129, 130, 153,
    198
in/on, 120
Intensive pronouns, 64, 71
Interjections, 2, 17

Intransitive verbs, 36
Irregular verbs, 28, 30
    principal parts of, 29
Italics for titles of longer works, 78
its, it's, 97

L

lay, lie, 35
Linking verbs, 2, 36, 37
Literature, present tense in writing
        about, 26
loose, lose, 97

M

Main clauses, 111, 132, 133, 156, 167
    in complex sentences, 167, 175, 184
    in compound-complex sentences,
        167, 179, 184
    in compound sentences, 167, 171,
        184
    in simple sentences, 167, 184
Mechanics, 21, 104
Misplaced modifiers, 145, 158
Modifiers, 46, 158, 198. *See also*
        Adjective(s); Adverb(s)
    clauses as, 144
    dangling, 148–149, 158
    misplaced, 145, 158
    phrases as, 144
    possessive pronouns as, 60

N

Negatives, 56
    double, 56, 71, 105
no less than, subject-verb agreement
        and, 32
Noncount nouns, 42, 43
Noun(s), 2
    abstract, 39
    collective, 40–41
    concrete, 39, 42
    count, 42, 43
    defined, 39
    infinitives used as, 128
    noncount, 42, 43
    proper, 2
    spelling plurals of, 92
    use of verbals as, 122
    using, as adjectives, 14
Noun clauses, 137, 138, 156
    words introducing, 137, 175
nowhere, 57
Numbers, 99

O

Objective case pronouns, 60, 61
Objects
    compound, 2
    objective case pronouns used as, 60
    of preposition, 2
on/in, 120

P

Parallel structure, 9
Participial phrases, 125–126, 127, 153,
        198

Participle, 126, 198
    past, 26, 36, 125
    present, 125
Parts of speech, 1, 2. *See also specific*
Past participle, 26, 36, 125
Past perfect progressive tense, 23
Past perfect tense, 22
Past progressive tense, 23
Past tense, 22, 36
Periods with quotation marks, 80
Personal pronouns, 59, 71
    objective case, 60, 61
    plural, 59
    possessive case, 60
    singular, 59
    subjective case, 59
Personal titles, abbreviations for, 99
Personification, 16
Phrases, 111, 112, 153, 199
    adjective, 113–114, 153
    adverb, 115, 153
    gerund, 123–124, 130, 153
    infinitive, 128–129, 130, 153
    participial, 125–126, 127, 153
    prepositional, 111, 112, 117, 153
    verbal, 111, 122, 123
Plural nouns, spelling, 92
Plural pronoun, 41
Plural verb, 41
plus, subject-verb agreement and, 32
Poetry, using capitalization to write
        about, 86
Positive degree of comparison, 50, 51,
        71, 198
Possessive case pronouns, 60
Predicate, 199
Preposition(s), 2, 112
    common, 7–8, 112
    object of, 2
    troublesome, 120
Prepositional phrases, 111, 112, 117,
        153, 199
    as adjective, 113–114
    as adverb, 115
    commas after, 79
Present participle, 26, 125
Present perfect progressive tense, 23
Present perfect tense, 22
Present progressive tense, 23
Present tense, 22, 23, 26
Pronouns, 2, 59
    agreement with antecedent, 62, 71
    indefinite, 65–66
    intensive, 64, 71
    personal, 59, 71
    reflexive, 63–64, 71
    relative, 139, 175
Proper adjectives, capitalization of, 84
Proper nouns, capitalization of, 2, 84
Punctuation, 77–78. *See also specific*

Q

Quantifiers, 47, 48
Question marks, with quotation marks,
        81
quiet, quite, 97

Quotation(s), capitalization of first word
        in, 84
Quotation marks
    commas with, 80
    in dialogue, 81
    to enclose direct quotations, 78
    exclamation points with, 81
    periods with, 80
    question marks with, 81
    for titles of short works, 78

R

Reflexive pronouns, 63–64, 71
Regular verbs, 27
Relative pronouns, 139, 175

S

Salutation, capitalization of words in, 84
Semicolons
    in forming compound sentences, 77,
        171
    in series, 77
Sentence(s), 175
    capitalization of first word in, 84
    complex, 167, 175, 178, 179, 184
    compound, 167, 171, 172, 174, 179,
        184
    compound-complex, 167, 179, 184
    parts of, 199
    simple, 167, 168, 170, 184
Sentence fragments, 136
set, sit, 35
Sexist language, 63
Similes, 105
Simple sentences, 167, 168, 170, 184,
        199
sit, set, 35
somewhere, 57
Spelling
    of difficult words, 97
    list of frequently misspelled words,
        95
    rules of, 90, 91, 92
        adding of prefixes, 90
        adding of suffixes, 90
        doubling of final consonant, 90
        final *e* before consonant, 90
        final *e* before vowel, 90
        final *y* preceded by consonant, 90
        i before *e,* 90
        plurals of nouns, 92
        rules of, 91, 92
    using dictionary for, 98
Subjective case pronouns, 59
Subjects, 199
    agreement with verb, 30–33
    compound, 32, 33, 61, 168
    subjective case pronouns used as,
        59
Subordinate clauses, 111, 132, 134,
        137, 156, 167
    in complex sentences, 167, 175, 184
    in compound-complex sentences,
        167, 179, 184
    who in, 139
    words that introduce, 175

Subordinate conjunctions, 141, 175
Superlative degree of comparison, 50, 51, 71, 198

T

take, bring, 35
Tense, 199. *See also under* Verbs
than, then, 97
that there, 57
their, there, they're, 97
then, than, 97
there, their, they're, 97
this here, 57
Titles, capitalization of first and main words in, 84
together with, subject-verb agreement and, 32
too, to, 97
Transitive verbs, 36
Travel writing, using capitalization in, 88

U

Underlining for titles of longer works, 78
until/by, 120

Usage, 21

V

Verbal phrases, 111, 122, 123
Verbals, 111, 122
Verbs, 2, 199
    action, 2, 36
    agreement with subject, 30–33
    compound, 168
    helping, 26
    intransitive, 36
    irregular, 28, 30
        principal parts of, 29
    linking, 2, 36, 37
    principal parts of, 26
    regular, 27
    tense of, 22
        future, 22
        future perfect, 22
        future perfect progressive, 23
        future progressive, 23
        past, 22, 36
        past perfect, 22
        past perfect progressive, 23

        past progressive, 23
        present, 22, 23, 26
        present perfect, 22
        present perfect progressive, 23
        present progressive, 23
        staying with same, 24
    transitive, 36
    troublesome, 34–35
        principal parts of, 35

W

wear, where, 97
weather, whether, 97
where, wear, 97
whether, weather, 97
who, in subordinate clauses, 139
with, subject-verb agreement and, 32
Words
    frequently misspelled, 95
    often confused, 97

Y

you, subject-verb agreement and, 33
you're, your, 97